WANDERING BETWEEN TWO WORLDS

ESSAYS ON FAITH AND ART

ANITA MATHIAS

Published by Benediction Books, Oxford

Published by

Benediction Books
11 Kiln Lane,
Garsington,
Oxford,
OX44 9AR
United Kingdom
Email: **benedictionbooks@btinternet.com**

Copyright 2007 Anita Mathias
First Edition First Printing 2007

The right of Anita Mathias to be identified as the author of this
work has been asserted by her in accordance with the Copyright,
Designs and Patents Act, 1988.

A CIP Record for this book is available from the British
Cataloguing in Publication Data Office.

ISBN-10   0-9553737-0-0
ISBN-13   978-0-9553737-0-1

Printed by Biddles Ltd.,
24 Rollesby Road, Hardwick Industrial Estate, King's Lynn,
Norfolk PE30 4LS

Set in Adobe Jenson Pro 11pt/13pt and Adobe Garamond Pro
8pt & 9.6pt

WANDERING BETWEEN TWO WORLDS
Essays on Faith and Art

Acknowledgments

White Elephants and **The Winters of the Matriarchs** were originally published "That Ancient Yarn," in *The Virginia Quarterly Review*, and won a National Endowments for the Arts Award.

Zigzags was published as "Memories of a Catholic Childhood," *Commonweal*, and in *The Best Spiritual Writing 2000*, HarperSanFrancisco.

The Holy Ground of Kalighat was published in *Notre Dame Magazine* and in *The Best Spiritual Writing, 1999*, HarperSanFrancisco.

Aliens and Strangers *Southwest Review, Volume 87, #2, Nov. 2002*.

Writing and Prayer was published in an earlier version as "Learning to Pray," in *The Christian Century*, March 22nd, 2000. Reproduced in Religion Online.

First Thing in the Morning The Style Plus Page, The Washington *Post*, 16th September, 1997.

I am grateful to the National Endowment for the Arts and the Minnesota State Arts Board for individual artist grants. Thank you to Simon Farres for designing and type-setting the book.

This book is dedicated to Roy, Zoe and Irene Mathias with gratitude for their love and support.

1 | White Elephants

In Bombay, *goondas* speed up to auto-rickshaws, then lean over to yank dangling earrings. If the passenger's ear rips, it rips. *Never* wear jewelry in Bombay: This Sindhi, in the latest *Blitz*, laid her arm, *glittering* with gold bangles, on the open window of her car. Men with machetes drove beside her on a dark road, then sped away holding her arm on which those bangles still glittered. Ice-lollies sold by pushcart men are made from filthy water scooped from gutters. "How are they to get municipal water in those cardboard and rag squatter shacks, you tell me now?" Shammi kebabs sold on sidewalks are rotting dead dog, not lamb. "Lamb, huh! As if they'd sell lamb!" Those circus children who soar, spangly and sequined, were, of course, kidnapped. A chloroform-soaked handkerchief slides across the faces of children who stray, you know, just down the road from their parents. Sometimes, their legs are sliced mid-thigh, so they look piteous as they beg crouched on their little skateboards, their masters watching in the shadows, eyes narrowed on the take. This beggar, in *The Bombay Herald*, died with a *lakh* of rupees sewn into his mattress; *some in rags, and some in bags, and some in velvet gowns*. If you take a taxi late at night, the cabbie aimlessly zigzags through the city, or if he sees you are a *buddhu*, drives around in circles, quite shamelessly grinning at the meter. Sometimes passengers *vanish*. And wash up out of the Arabian Sea, sans watch, sans wallet, throat slit. Unaccompanied female women are abducted to brothels at Falkland Road – "Did you see those Illustrated Weekly pictures?" – to join the sad prostitutes in their cages.

My grandmother said so. My mother said so.

"But what are brothels?"

"Never you mind."

And never mind that Nana never left her Catholic suburb of Bandra for big bad Bombay; in fact, rarely left her own home: drunken bus drivers, bogeymen, beggar-men, thieves. "The drivers these days, maniacs! Bought their driver's license with a bribe; couldn't be bothered about pedestrians; expect you to run out of their way; how can *I* run? It's no longer safe to cross a street in Bombay," Nana said with finality.

We called my grandmother, Molly, Small Nana, not just because she was as diminutive and cute as a doll, which – timid and diffident, four feet something, in her perennial mid-calf batik dresses – she was, or because, as a child might, she served almost everything: sliced beetroot, tomato, pineapple, melon, rice, mutton curry, pancakes, or buttered toast with a frosting of the sugar forbidden her, a diabetic. It was to distinguish her from Big Nana, Alice Rebello, her mother, my great-grandmother, frail, mild, with a constant gentle smile who, miraculously on every visit, slipped my mother an exquisite piece of jewelry for us "when we grew up," delicate confections of diamonds, tiny rubies and pearls, or large Burma rubies with sparkling deep depths set in rings and earrings bought for her in Persia by my great-grandfather, a veterinary surgeon, attending the British army, or, more precisely, its horses. ("Horse-doctor's granddaughter," we'd tease my mother, forgetting our two degrees of connection.) These Big Nana slipped to us when unobserved by her son and daughter-in-law, who had moved in with her, an ex-nun of whom my father said, "She's a virago." ("What is a virago?" "Oh never mind." Another word for my childhood Kabbalah: What are Free Masons? What is a Cabaret?– the flashing neon words over pictures of dancing girls divesting, whispered by my classmates: "Daddy went to *the cabaret*.") Jewelry so beautiful, and atavistically desired in a culture in which, traditionally, jewelry was a woman's only inalienable possession, yet with the power to rend relationships as it rent the earth in its emergence – for one might possess children in multiples, but not jewelry, so every piece given to Petra renders Paulina bitter, for jewelry – like food – represents love in the heart's secret algebra.

In dawning enlightenment, Nana realized she need never leave home. Within it, she had all she wanted: husband, children, and friends who'd drop in with the sweets she craved, delectable hemlock. And so she lived contentedly, in narrowing circles, a life-long voluntary house arrest, gradually renouncing visiting, parties, shopping, cooking, her world shrinking to ever fewer rooms.

And in this small world of family, in an odd transmutation, *she* became the child to be petted and indulged. My sister tricked Nana so often that, surely, she was counter-tricked. Eating a delicacy specially prepared for her, brain cutlets, tongue curry, she'd say, "Nana, this food is not nice." "And Nana's face fell," she'd crow. "And then I said 'It is *Delicious*.'" (She'd wave her hand in front of her mouth in agony, crying, "*It's hot*." "Fire-hot or chili-hot?" they'd ask, leaning forward solicitously). And so, protected, Nana floated, so passive she could never remember to cut her toe-nails; they grew, long, yellow, ridged, gnarled keratin, until the doctor paid a home-visit to cut them for her.

But faith can move mountains, and love can move recluses. Nana's two exceptions: Family, God. She left the house on rare and select missions: to visit her mother, Alice, or her grandmother, Flora Coelho (who, in a confusion-inducing swirl of modifiers, was my great-great-grandmother, still alive in my early childhood, famous for her fourteen children, "The Holy Family," of whom nine became nuns or Jesuits of outstanding piety – "the ginger beards," a stray Portuguese gene tinting their beards auburn – while her married children produced a slew of eminent churchmen and church-women.) Another exception: when her youngest son Reynald treated us to chop suey, sweet 'n sour, and vast cloying pastries in Bandra's sophisticated, upper-crusty MacRonnels whose green-lit and aromatic ambience made you hungry the instant you entered. Reynald, a Chartered Accountant, sweet-natured, gentle, smiley, was everyone's favorite, the frequent prerogative of the youngest; the only brother who did marry, late, he still, straight after work, visited his old home, where he was loved-up, lapped-up, listened to (and the never-seen characters of his office, like his lame polio-stricken boss, Patrick Saldanha, who never missed a day's work, transport strike, monsoon floods, or riots and their fires, provided life-extending, soap-operatic gratifications to his parents and his spinster sister Joyce) before he dragged himself to his own home, tired and talked-out, on the days he had the energy to.

The final exception: the perilous Sunday morning crossing of the street to the massive St. Andrew's Church, opposite her house, its floor, gravestones of glorious mismatched marble – deep peacock purple; pale green onion slices; dark red tree-rings, or the calm of sheerest white – a paving of crazy geometry, color and good intentions, bleating belated praises to generations of Coelhos, Rebellos, Lobos, Saldanhas and Noronhas, all of whom, apparently, were dearly beloved paragons, exemplary husbands and fathers, wives and mothers, and if those engraved lauds and laurels were a quarter-true, the final musing would be all too true, "The earth shall not see their like again." And in the courtyard, amid amiable huge-winged marble angels and antique urns, the oceanside family grave in which my elder brother Gerard, who died as an infant three days old, was buried, a spot of fascination, yet dread of the inevitable unruly adult emotion.

On Mondays, I returned with my aunt Joyce and her friend Laura to St. Andrew's to count the Sunday collection, tens of thousands of rupees, the mite of widows, paupers, princes, golden lads and lasses… The gleam and chink of money! Engineering feats: towers of pentagonal five paise coins; hexagonal twenties with Asoka's lions; round rupee coins, and eleven-sided twos. I counted in paise, my aunt in *annas*, six paise, a superseded unit my mother's family clove to, despite our decimalized post-Independence currency, counting in four and eight annas rather than twenty-five and fifty paise, to the confusion of children and vendors whose sweet transactions entailed such change. And when the Parish wanted money: Housie: *jaldi* five; two fat ladies, 88; one and six, sweet 16; all the sixes, 66; hockey sticks, 77; top of the house, 90, and sudden jubilation – Housie!

Aunt Joyce's dress was the perennial deep-frozen length of Bandra, in which, like an enchanted sleeping kingdom, fashions never changed. Christian women wore one-piece dresses ending just above the knee, a length unchanged from the Raj – right though the fifties when most grown women, my father's sisters, for instance, shed their anyway unbecoming dresses for saris, for now exposing your legs ("bacon and eggs," the cognoscenti said in Cockney rhyming slang) suggested you might be Anglo-Indian (who, the British gone, were now, by popular consensus, considered the progeny of the Saturday night flings of English Tommies and Indian maids).

Her hair hung lank, her make-up was perfunctory, her figure had thickened; as a young girl, however, Joyce had been pretty. At proposals from the most eligible bachelors, she had sobbed, "but I don't want to leave Mummy." Others came from rich men who, when the Portuguese began to convert our ancestral town of Mangalore nearly five centuries ago, had not, unlike my grandparents, been Brahmins. (The Brahmins, the most influential caste, had been converted first, with each extended family given a Portuguese surname, so that even today, surnames are a rough, though not infallible, guide to caste and class; and, anyway, the community remembers). My grandfather was aghast, "How can you even consider it? Centuries of *dirt* flowing in his veins!" And so Joyce remained in the house of her youth, a dragonfly in amber, nervous, harassed by the day's Sisyphean worries, whom I remember like a cautionary tale when I shiver on the shores of the great river.

* * *

"And here comes The Ma-ha-ra-ja," the middle brother Mervyn drawled – rolling the syllables in gleeful mockery, his voice suave, resonant, rich-timbered as port or Christmas cake, the voice of a born priest. His oldest brother, Eustace (an anomaly in that family of the worried) appeared, grinning, raffish as Rhett Butler in *Gone with the Wind* whom he resembled down to the ironic glint in his languid, heavy-lidded, deceptively sleepy eyes and his debonair mustache. The nick-name, with the truth encrypted in nick-names that take – was a not inapt description of Eustace's free-spending care-freeness and careless largesse, his flamboyance, his popularity, his indulgence of his family, his friends, and himself

– though inspired by the logo of Air India at which Eustace was a senior executive: an endomorphic, red-turbanned Maharaja, in an outmoded sherwani and red-striped, plumed turban, deeply bowing, on his mystic flying carpet, his courtly right angle bow to all hoi polloi with a plane ticket.

On Bombay evenings, Uncle Eustace took me to sit amid flashy acrobatic insects on the verandahs of his laughing friends, Lourdes with dyed orange hair, one leg amputated, the other swollen with elephantiasis; Helen – of Troy, inevitably – with a white poodle and a crisp pseudo-English accent which slowly faded; and giggly Dennis, his best friend and drinking partner – called, of course, "Dennis the Menace." He introduced me to the company with pride and apparent seriousness, "This is my niece, Anita. She goes to St. Mary's Convent, Nainital," and "Oooh, an India-famous school!" someone might say with only slightly mock awe, and, as befitted someone who went to an India-famous school, I was, in half-jest, offered a drink, which, as befitted someone who went to an India-famous school, I accepted in nonchalant earnest, "Yes, I think I'll have a shandy," I drawled. "Say, when." "When!" I said smartly as they filled the gag beer mugs past 3 fl oz. for a lady, 6 oz. for a gentlemen, almost up to the 9 oz. mark, marked *PIG*.

"What's your net worth, Edward? How much have you saved? What man, let us invest it for you," they said as his eyes grew dreamy, benevolent, cat-and-creamy. Or "Can you lend five hundred rupees? Unexpected expense...will return soon." All evening, banter – "Oh come off it, men," arm-pushing, back-slapping hilarity until your cheeks ached with the continual smiling at the continual badinage – except when you escaped into wine-red depths, which everyone, including I, did. And so after an evening of *shandy*, beer and lemonade; *toddy*, fermented coconut juice; *feni*, moonshine distilled from cashew nuts; or very sweet homemade mulberry wine (which we never considered considering alcohol), I returned, effusive, expansive, in love with the world and everything in it, and most of all with my own cleverness, and how brilliant were my bubbling bon mots. "Anita!" my mother, grandmother, and Aunt Joyce cried in unison. "Oh," I said airily, swaying, and not just because of my new high-heeled shoes, "I can hold my liquor," (an expression I'd picked up in those evenings). And everyone cried

"Eustace!" while he grinned, his mischievous dancing eyes half-closed and far away. *For he on honey-dew hath fed/ And drunk the milk of Paradise.*

At Lent, however, Eustace and his friends, Catholics all, together went on a preached retreat, thought of God, their souls, and the fires of hell, and renounced the sparkling spirits, which brought them sparkle and relaxation, and were the bedrock of their friendship, forswore all spirits but the Holy One, for the forty days of Lent and forever and ever after that – or least until bubbly Easter.

Eustace's lanky, skinny father, Stanislaus, also remembered, all too well, the dusty gloom of Ash Wednesday, Holy Day of Fast and Abstinence, first of the Lenten forty. So: anticipatory pangs well before Shrove Tuesday, when he returned, freshly shriven, to Mangalorean pancakes filled with freshly grated tender coconut in a date-palm jaggery syrup – which preemptively used all the butter, eggs, and milk in the house, increasing the odds of a spartan Lent.

Stanny said, "Oh Molly, make a few sannas for Shrove Tuesday," (fluffy, discus shaped, steamed rice-flour dumplings, with no Western correlative). "Oh, and a little pork vindaloo with that, Molly," and (forgetting he had asked for sannas) "appas," (toddy-risen flatbreads) "and your mutton and lentil curry, Molly, the godachi mutli. And coconut and bimli (a uniquely tasteless squash – one of India's vegetables, like ambade and tamarind, which grow on trees!) And your beef with grated coconut goes with bimli. Will you be able to make Chicken Indas, Molly; we'll be fasting all Wednesday, and perhaps pole (rice pancakes) with it …?" Thus fortified, he set his face like flint for Ash Wednesday, keeping a word-perfect fast, as well he might.

Ironically, Uncle Mervyn, larger each year, physically resembled the Air India Maharaja. His big, round beaming face had a polished sheen; his large, lustrous, slightly squinted eyes sparkled at his own sardonic murmurings; he was always at home, comfy in his trademark T-shirt and baggy Bermuda shorts, shrouded in the nimbus of the "self-employed."

51 Chimbai Road: The front door, spirals of wrought iron over wood with flaking paint, opened onto a foyer where, behind those screens with which Indians, like Japanese, create new rooms, Uncle Mervyn, a self-employed stock-broker, worked – not entirely an overstatement, for, sporadically though the day, little old Catholic ladies in their immutable Bandra shapeless flowery dresses, visited with anxious portfolios inherited from fathers, bachelor brothers, or dead husbands: tenuous lifelines, everything hinging on the prompt passage of their dividends through the chancy arteries of the mail. The mail, the mail man, objects of sad, strained aquiline eyes. Bandra's Boggart took the shape of bags of mail floating on monsoon flooded streets, washed out from alley refuse heaps into which they'd been dumped on bored and lazy days. ("Has TISCO sent you your dividend?" "I haven't received my dividend from Glaxo.")

A commute down the corridor, work from home, set your own hours – glamorous, alluring lures. Once a month, however, Mervyn, scrubbed and glowing in his dazzling starched terrycot shirt and pants, a strand of long hair pulled over his balding head; his huge, hazel eyes bulging with importance as his briefcase was with paperwork to be filed in person, and in triplicate – got ready for his tram ride to the Stock Exchange at Bombay, while his mother and sister clucked admonition around him. Though Bandra *was* Bombay to us, to my grandparents, inveterate homebodies, the commute from the safe suburb to Bombay, den of iniquity, nest of vipers, sepulcher of the righteous, great Gomorrah was nasty, fraught, and rare, dreaded in inverse proportion to its frequency: goondas, accidents, murders, muggings. "But Nana, *everyone* doesn't get murdered, robbed or kidnapped," I reasoned, reasonably. "Why should we?" "Why shouldn't you?" they asked, their bleak law of probability. And the fact that my father was pick-pocketed – three times – when he went to Bombay, and that we, invariably, got ourselves lost, and once, in our haste to catch the subway, jumped into a first class compartment with a second class ticket, and were heavily fined – unreceipted – did not increase her confidence in us, or in the monster city.

Sanctity, they say, has an aroma, the fragrance of roses around the corpse of Francis Xavier, or Padre Pio; so too does sadness, so too does failure. Molecules of its mournful cologne mouldered on Uncle Mervyn. Perhaps this scent of sadness came from the leaching of life's romances – both minor: the romance of travel, the romance of reading *everything*, of the achievement of ambition, of, say, "writing a book," and major: parent love, erotic love, the love of God. When his siblings mocked his early yearning to become a priest, his secret celebration of improvised masses with missal, bell, candles, censer, and liturgical Latin, he gravitated towards the most common default romance: Money, the bracken, the brush, the wilderness, the weeds that cloaks our saddest ruins – abandoned dreams.

Food and money, ancient Biblical idols. Money, the commonest collection; food, the commonest comfort. As steaming savory mirages drifted into Mervyn's memory, he dialed one of his genteel neighborhood friends with more time than money. At lunch, for a small fee, his fantasies lay incarnated before us through the conjurations of Edith, a serious, middle-aged lady, with a neat shoulder-length perm, cat's eyes glasses and tight-sashed floral dresses: the Anglo-Indian cuisine we thought of as English, but which I have never encountered in England (or anywhere else!): "potato chops" – mashed potato croquettes, fried in egg and bread-crumbs, stuffed with spicy minced beef; or "pan rolls," crepes with a minced meat filling, fried golden with bread crumb bristles, an East-West fusion for our mildly Westernized palates.

Or sometimes, sarpatel, archetypal Mangalorean delicacy, chunks of pork beneath inches of fat and chewy, rubbery rind, simmered in a sauce of spices, wine and blood. A shibboleth. "Is your father Mangalorean?" a wedding hostess asked as I got him refills while he chuckled over the lyrics floating from the house where the bride was bathed in coconut milk for her roce, her wedding shower, while her friends sung the saddest, oddest dirges, until she cried: Good Luck! "Oh, you poor thing," they sang. "That mother-in-law! When you visit her, she'll be vegetarian; when she's visits you, she'll be non-vegetarian. Her visits will be almost eternal. When she leaves, so will your most precious possessions." "Good, he's Mangalorean," the hostess said, freely loading his plate.

"Then he loves sarpatel." My near-vegetarian father nearly wailed. He eschewed pork: free-ranging, gutter-feeding, its tape-worm spreading meningitis, its round worm causing the recent epidemic of encephalitis.

Mervyn eschewed water with equal rigor, drinking only Mangola, expensive, sweetened bottled mango juice. When the neighborhood's illiterate Koli fisher-families sent their sons to the house for help in getting a job or decoding their bank passbook, he'd drawl, "Fetch me a crate of Mangola," his voice full-bodied, luscious, ripe-fruity, and slip an extra fiver into their hands, noblesse oblige. "The lakhpati!" my aunt Joyce exclaimed. "He behaves like a lakhpati. Give me what you give them; I'll be a lakhpati too." (A lakh, a hundred thousand rupees – like a crore, ten million – is a uniquely Indian unit, necessary in an inflationary economy. For all Joyce's teasing, Mervyn, who never worked a regular job, died with a collection of them.)

Over lunch, my father and Uncle Mervyn twirled crystal Maharaja-engraved champagne goblets of Mangola, inhaled the bouquet of fizzy wealth, drunk deep. I listened – stocks, bonds, dividends, while the accountant regions of my mind calculated along: double your money in seven years at ten percent with Binny's, but with Larsen and Toubro, double your money in five years at fifteen percent, but with more risk. I planned, importantly, to explode my own little nest egg with the miracle of compound interest (100 rupees, 110, 121, 133; ten percent at the rule of 72, too slow, let's try…) hearing the tick-tock of money being fruitful, implacably increasing and multiplying. Oh, I'd become a millionaire off the abundance encoded in creation for the diligent and imaginative – encrypted in a single tomato seed (plant, plants: farm); an egg (a chicken, eggs: a chicken empire). "I know what, Ma. I'll have a fudge stall at school; you cook the fudge, and I'll…." "Your head I will!" But, always, I'd back off from this obsession, heady in its wild mathematics, its astrophysical immensity – but, so what? For what? Oh, I'd be a millionaire too, I decided, airily. *All things are possible*: childhood's birthright.

Mervyn's magic: He'd suddenly appear with a gigantic brown paper bag from which, with magicianly panache, he produced chocolate – Krisp, Five Star, Gems, Caramello, Bournville,

Cadbury's Raisin, or Fruit and Nut, which, beaming with the pleasure of magnanimity, he bestowed on us, *voila*, responding to my little sister's delirious delight – "Wow, Uncle *Mervyn*!" – with an almost eternal "There's more, baby doll!" until finally, almost incredibly, he came to the last loaf, the last fish, and even our gluttonous eyes realized, without sadness, that there was no more.

Food and money, ancient idols, food, money and the news. As the cocky pre-dawn chanticleers competed with the muezzin to awake the dawn, Mervyn's radio's purred while he monitored the world with *The Blitz*, *The Bombay Herald*, *The Times of India* and the morning coffee, each addiction equally potent. Bribery, corruption, politicians and other crooks, and the unnerving rise to power of the Shiv Sena who wanted Bombay renamed Mumbai, for heaven's sake, and a Hindustan for Hindus – as if those rooted in the land through race, and immemorial residence should belong any less to it because of a private faith adopted fuzzy centuries ago by fuzzy ancestors.

The grief of the world unfurled over the newspapery breakfasts Mervyn masterminded. From the neighborhood's only cold storage, the Koli boys fetched, in waxy cerements, the luxury meats of my childhood, ham, bacon, sausages, salami, luncheon meat. These were served with "Nana's scrambled eggs," the only thing she personally cooked, fried rich golden in *ghee*, with onion, coriander and mint. Eustace surveyed this gastronomic indulgence coolly, while he ate, or rather drank, standing up, his unvarying breakfast – two raw beaten eggs, which I found impossible to swallow despite my great admiration of his jauntiness.

All morning, in his office cluttered with cherished type-writers, and an expanding universe of shortwave radios, Mervyn twiddled knobs with fingers as compulsive as those bewitched by Rubik's cube, extracting flickering stations, the B. B. C; the Voice of America, and, most of all, jazzy Radio Ceylon so that he knew the lyrics of ABBA, Cliff Richards, or Simon and Garfunkel as well as the coolest girls at school. *And in the naked night, I saw/ Ten thousand people, maybe more. /People talking without speaking, /People hearing without listening, /People writing songs that voices never share/ And no one dare/Disturb the sound of silence.*

And now and again: Scoop! He knew, before the news, of the rescue of Israeli hostages in ninety minutes at Entebbe, and, closer to home, late one evening, he heard of the 757 wrecked on the beach three minutes away, and, of course, we scrambled over slippery algae-covered rocks and fishing nets spread out to dry, arriving at the scene with the rescue workers, and behind the ropes that cordoned off the treacherous rocks and the sea from the curious and the greedy, watched them haul in the wrecked suitcases and bodies and the plucky rubber doll that bobbed above the waves.

The sea, the sea! It shimmered, rippling, corrugated silver. Sudden breezes brought the acrid, exhilarating hors d'oevry tang of the "bombay ducks," long, silvery fish, and *bhangra*, mackerel, the Koli fisherwoman sun-dried on the beach – making us forever hungry. "Yes, sea air makes you peckish," said our grandparents, delighted by slang (as knowing, as pleased, as the German nuns at my Himalayan boarding school were with *their* elemental dicta: "Mountain air makes you hungry") hungry even after the table at tea, brilliant with cloying sohn halwa from camel's milk, and orange, red, yellow and green "Bombay halwas" so rich that flecks of ghee, clarified butter, the creme de la crème, visibly oozed from their pores. Such, such were the joys of our holidays in Bombay.

Across the road, washed gold-silver by the setting sun, the ocean battered the sea-wall, beckoning, summoning; sea-gulls screeched on the wings of the wind; breakers and waves crashed as in the scarcely noticed background of a dream. Obstat, verboten, anathema. Couldn't go without them: kidnappers, speeders, and the never-voiced danger of rape. Couldn't go with them: inside, somnolence reigned. So, silver bells and cockle shells, we played in the long barren front yard, its soil, shells from ages past when all had been ocean-floor, or the Arabian Sea flooded it in a forgotten tidal wave. And after years of careful beach-combing, still: conch, wentletrap, periwinkle, whelk, shells that sang of ancient seas, aliens and strangers on the earth. "Look, Shalini, look; I found a joined shell." "But I found a green shell." "Huh! 'She sells sea shells on the sea shore. The sea shells that she sells are sea shore shells.' Now you say it." She couldn't, though her teacher made her daily recite a lisp poem: "the ambitious Brussels sprout," until *ambississ* become a family expression of half-forgotten provenance.

Shells of mystery, shells of marvel, sirens of forbidden seas. We carted them into the house, returned, and still there were more, numberless as the descendants promised to Abraham – "as the stars in the sky and the sand in the seashore" – the latter, the most staggering metaphor for infinity, for in the sultry summer nights when we slept on the verandah, I, every night, attempted to count the stars to seduce sleep, and it seemed a doable enterprise, if one had patience and a system. Time moved slowly, the timeless time of childhood. When the sun dazed us, we drifted indoors to gaze absently at the pretty-pretty ceramic tiles on the window sills: an English cottage near a watermill; a plump-cheeked English girl, her hair spilling from her headband, framing her face, her cheek against a puppy; or sit cross-legged in the dark, lace-curtained living room examining the treasures in my grandfather's display cabinet, an ostrich egg, a delicate blue and gold doll's china tea set; bowls of rose-colored Bohemian crystal, or monogrammed, filigreed silver – while hours passed in the delusive eternity of childhood. At my back, I did not hear time's winged chariot drawing near, and had I – I would have leapt into it!

Among the antiques, the beloved, soon-captured book of Master Plots, which I read and re-read – old supplanted classics, *Lavengro*, *Lorna Doone*, *The Cloister and the Hearth*, about the parents of Erasmus, for heaven's sake; sad French novels, *Pere Goriot*, *Eugenie Grandet* full of the misery of miserliness, an apt derivation; and *Madame Bovary* dead, black arsenic streaming from her lovely mouth. I desultorily picked others up, entrenching a habit of dipping: G.K. Chesterton's *The Everlasting Man*, my grandparents' wedding present; and Victorians, eminent and otherwise: a biography of Alfred, Lord Tennyson, by his son, Hallam; Lord Macaulay, William Cobbett (who's he?), undergraduate best student prizes in English literature that my grandfather, Stanislaus, had won at the Jesuit Saint Aloysius' College in Mangalore in 1912, 1913, and 1914.

My tall, lanky, straight-backed grandfather, Stanislaus, wore the small black-rimmed glasses and baggy tweed trousers and jacket which were the trademark of old gentlemen of his school, and had the long, sunken, suffering face of T. S. Eliot, to whom he bore an uncanny resemblance. Stanny, like my father, could recite long passages of poetry, Milton, Wordsworth, Coleridge, Keats or Tennyson right into his seventies, when he died. Inheriting their ability to memorize easily, almost unconsciously, I learnt snatches of poems, which were then, to me, mere music, sonnets such as *The world is too much with us; late and soon,/Getting and spending, we lay waste our powers*. Milton's majestic periodic music was also indelibly imprinted on my father's neurons; once he started declaiming, it flowed, mellifluous honey: *Of Man's first disobedience, and the fruit/ Of that forbidden tree whose mortal taste/ Brought death into the world, and all our woe,/ With loss of Eden…/ Sing, Heav'nly Muse.*

But that mortal taste – entropy, the path of least resistance that makes men and streams crooked, the blight that drives to forbidden fruit – wrought what Emerson calls a crack in creation, exiled us from the magic kingdom of heaven, interplanted thorns and thistles in the Champs Elysees of work, our sweat dripping into the cursed recalcitrant dust unto which, unoriginally, we shall return.

The Biblical trio of tempters: the flesh, the devil, and the world that is too much with us, insidiously choking with busyness and distraction the life of the mind, no less than of the spirit. In another world, another time, my grandfather, gentle, unworldly, nervous, would have been a scholar, but he had twelve siblings, and his father, a land-owner, had lost his land after standing surety for a friend. A man in such a position was expected to earn his living after a first degree (like my early-orphaned father, decades later, who did time decoding classified telegrams in the British Embassy in Afghanistan, before England and his professional degree.) So Stanny bartlebyied his way to the Customs House, eventually becoming Collector of Customs and a much-sought expert in the arcana of the Customs Law of the British Empire, and then of independent India.

And so – overwhelmed by the sad necessity, before women worked, for even the most impractical man to provide for his wife and children – my grandfather who could sweetly and wistfully recite *In Xanadu did Kubla Khan a stately pleasure dome decree* (perhaps with the grief that precludes being "just friends" after a shattered romance) gave up reading, abandoning the struggle to find a quiet spot, a quiet hour, in a house with a wife and five children, and tides of Porlockian friends seeking help and solace and to beguile an empty hour, his creativity now confined to long spidery letters with quirky pen and ink drawings, and infallible recipes like chocolate snowball surprise: mould melted chocolate, condensed milk, desiccated coconut into balls. Though seeing me leaf through his books – "I'll teach you to love poetry," he'd say happily.

The living room: lace curtains drawn, dusky, drowsy with lotus-eating languor – *"a land in which it seemed always afternoon. And all round the coast, the languid air did swoon."* Trying to get something done was like swimming through treacle. So, naturally, one never rid the corners of rooms of dust-striped, tigerish paper piles of delusive good intentions: half-read *Eve's Weeklys* and *Feminas*; clippings clipped who knows when, who knows why, and for who knows whom; and skimmed letters to be re-read and destroyed, whose illicit enchantment I rarely resisted, and, besides, the layered midden of generations, old silver, old china, old cut glass, fragile old jewelry, too treasured, too precious to use, all fearsomely tagged – "of sentimental value." When he wished to destroy, we were told, the King of Siam sent a glorious white elephant – too sacred to work, an insult to give away – whose upkeep devoured one's life. White elephants, white elephants everywhere.

The integrity of my grandfather was commented on in the Catholic and secular press after his death, so there was not the blind eye, the murmured word, the friend-of-my-friendship which lubricates Indian life, just honest advice on honest circumnavigation to friends, and the friends of friends – who remembered him at Divali with gift boxes of dried fruit and chocolates, ties and tie-pins, crystal vases and clocks, and at Christmas, when my grandfather's house was the place to be. These gifts, in their original boxes, piled up above cupboards, under beds or lacy table-cloths, full measure, pressed down, flowing over from heaps and stacks, until my grandparents were imprisoned by their own abundance.

So, like the hobbits or Japanese, they indefatigably exchanged never-used gifts, *mathoms* in Hobbitish; electric sandwich-makers and cuff links, ash-trays and tea-trays, vanity cases and brief cases recirculated around the inner circle, or – awaiting resurrection at wedding, christening, or birthday – moldered in large steel almirahs along with their carefully folded wrapping paper, bows, and ribbons. Abundance can be as oppressive as poverty, but neither compare with the guilty oppressions of thrift.

I returned to Jamshedpur with a old suitcase, given by Uncle Eustace who had given up traveling, full of old books, with fading cloth binding but still inviting gilt titles, over which I cried, *Adam Bede, Silas Marner,* or off-the-beaten-track Hardy, *The Trumpet Major* and *Two on a Tower,* prize books, text books, the books of their youth, given to me by those who had given up reading, my aunt's friends, Laura and Chrissie (along with guilty advice: always look up an unfamiliar word, and, soon, you'll rarely meet a word you don't know) and – a college degree in English literature being a tradition in my mother's family – books *ex libris* my mother's brothers and sisters, her cousin, Marjorie, her father, Stanislaus, and my grandmother, Molly, who, surprisingly for one so timid, was among the first Indian women to study at a co-educational college, the Jesuit St. Xavier's in Bombay (achieving effortlessly, with one learned colonial leap, the college education to which English proto-feminists had recently won the right).

In Bandra, I was known as "the girl who's always reading," "who writes so beautifully," and much faded hope and withered longing was displaced onto me by family and their friends who out of Saharas of shriveled ambition, the sky now out of limits, cheered me on as they pointed to bright and morning stars they no longer pursued. So many relatives we visited, confronted by the megalopolis, had made peace with small lives, and with an apparent lack of restlessness, and a sad surrender of aspiration, just lived to live, each tomorrow the same, creeping in a petty pace.

Is ambition indeed "the last infirmity of noble minds?" Or is it the force that through the green fuse drives the flower, the wine of life, both path and north star through trackless wastes of desert days? The boat that swirls you from bogs and swamps into the great river.

One still had ambition. My grandfather's nephew, Albert. Everyone had a back-story, painted with a fine brush on two inches of ivory, rosetta clue to everything; Albert's was the story (true? false?) of his irate mother marching in to the office to berate her husband in front of his colleagues. And he, highly-strung, too shamed to return, wandered daily by the river, by the weeping willows, an objective correlative. A slip of the foot, of the will? *Those are pearls that were his eyes. Of his bones are coral made.*

Auden, in a complicated genetic diagram, shows how a nephew can be the true descendant of an uncle in temperament, physique, gifts, all that matters. That was certainly true of my grandfather and Albert, who, brilliant and spiritual as none of his own sons were, was sent, by his diocese to study in the Pontifical Seminary at Rome.

He returned to pay his beloved uncle a surprise visit. Surprises! A self-indulgence, cheating the putative beneficiary of the joy of anticipation. Sometimes dangerously.

My grandfather shuffled to the doorbell. *Albert!* His hand to his heart. A mild stroke; a heart attack? The doctor, summoned, said, "You'll have to have an ECG, Mr. Coelho." "An ECG?" he protested. "I had one in 1954."

"The doctor looked at him quizzically," my grandmother said. "They knew he had a very good sense of humor. You could never tell if he was joking."

"Mr. Coelho, that was twenty years ago," the doctor said firmly. "The heart changes from minute to minute." A new much-quoted "famous last word," like the Jamshedpur tailor's stern pronouncement when my father protested against the suit my mother chose, "Sir, Madam knows best."

My father and I would go into Bombay after breakfast with an itinerary: purchases enjoined upon us by my mother; Juhu Beach; visit my father's cousins, Joy and Gladys. Our proud travelers' tales on our return resembled no blue-print: hunted for the perfect Chola Bhatura, saw *Anne of a Thousand Days...* For even pleasurable adventures, once planned, seem planned, a have-to, making me want to do something different, surprising even myself. "But, but, but…" spluttered my grandmother and Joyce. My father grinned, putting his tongue on his upper lip, a tic when extremely pleased with himself. "What to do?" he said. "A woman's mind changes from minute to minute."

Soon after Albert's visit, my grandfather died. Albert returned to Rome. Was never heard of or from. His sister in Kuwait offered rewards; there were sightings. Interpol helped. Fruitlessly. He had vanished – murdered, amnesic following a head injury, or, perhaps, in an unimaginable declaration of independence, he had slashed fraying Gordian cords, and reinvented himself.

* * *

51 Chimbai Road was an old house, its yellowing "white-wash" molting flakes that my sister and I surreptitiously peeled, poking their jagged edges beneath our finger-nails with a nervous pleasure in their sharpness. In the narrow strip behind the house and the high back walls, banana and papayas fell unharvested, their sweetness wasted. "He never accepted a bribe," my father said of his father-in-law. "And everyone else goes into customs only *for* the bribes," turning blind for a price while smugglers introduced gold, synthetic sarees, watches, perfume, western music, juicers, or the coveted "mixie-grinder" into India's protectionist markets.

"And so," he continued, "His colleagues own huge beach houses, but he still rents" – the lower floor of the rambling two storey house facing the sea, in which my mother was born. Their formidable old spinster landlady, Cissy (Cecilia) Valladares, lived in her lair on the upper floor of this house she'd inherited which – despite Bombay's rent control laws – provided her with a comfortable predictable income, and the consequent ironic fate of becoming one of those un/fortunate people whose days are black holes of infinite space with no Jacob's ladder of work across them.

When the Coelhos talked about her, as one talks about land-ladies, they metonymically spelled out UP, and so, with smarmy traditional manners, I called her Aunty Youpee, and a new code had to be invented. She had once blocked my path, her face, a scatter of warts and wens beneath her Medusa curls. "What mischief did you do that you got those?" she pointed at my violet-indigo tom-girls' face. I pointed up in turn, and asked, "What mischief did *you* do that *you* got those?" She gasped, my grandfather gasped, pulling me away, though he, shy, correct, unfailingly polite could barely conceal his merriment. "Anita!" my mother, grandmother and Aunt Joyce cried out. My grandfather said – proudly, "See what answers she gives at five. What answers will she give at twenty-five?" My father laughed gleefully.

Youpee stalked out increasingly infrequently until she no longer could. When I went up with Mervyn – her sole visitor – to read her the newspaper, the fearsome witch of my childhood lay helpless in her own excrement. Her around-the-clock ayahs malingered, squatting in the purer air of the balcony, absently sieving rice, far from her faint old woman voice. Her only relatives, three nieces, were invisible. We hollered, the ayah turned her over; the bed-sores on her bottom and back were chasms of pink raw flesh, almost reaching the bone.

She died, leaving the sprawling house to her now-visible nieces (that old, strange, stronger-than-water business) who in the Gotterdamerung that made the landscape of so many childhoods the landscape of memory, pulled down 51 Chimbai Road – a plummy location, opposite both the beach, and the huge St. Andrew's Church, nucleus of the suburb's Catholic social, cultural and religious life. Bayside went up in its stead (making them instant multi-millionaires) – twenty floors of apartments, no room now for quirky mansions with flaking paint. The old order yielded to lego block symmetries, boxy flats, to the left, to the right, on top of, below each other, two hundred families living in a patch of earth which had housed two. And in this world where neither the good nor the evil get quite what they deserve, the aunt, shunned alive, gave them, dead, munificence they could never have dreamed of, growing up in sleepy Bandra.

And, as compensation for their torn down rented house, my grandparents were given a free flat in the posh new Bayside:

a seaside residence, like their peers – through the interventions of providence and the current socialist legislation which protected long term tenants against radically raised rents or evictions – but without the stress, humiliations, and subterfuges of dishonesty. The wages of honesty: not so bad after all.

It was easy for your mind to change from minute to minute in gay Bombay, the polyglot music of its streets familiar from "Trade," the Indian Monopoly – Marine Drive, Chowpatty Beach, Cuffe Parade, Churchgate, Flora Fountain, Apollo Bunder, Malabar Hill; Bombay where we bought a year's supply of shawls, Punjabi gaghra cholis, churidars, shalwar kameez, jeans, mini, then midi shirts, shoes, nightdresses, and jewelry (for it had India's widest, wildest range from understated elegance to show-offy garishness). Bombay, to which all roads led, the country's delight, excitement throbbing through it like the Bollywood and Beatles songs from little stores with over-the-counter almost any food of the appetite's desiring: north Indian kulchas, south Indian uttapams, western Angels and Devils prancing on Horseback, tiny black seeds of caviar – and under-the-counter smuggled almost-anything in the warrens of smuggler's paradises like Bori Bunder or the covered Crawford market, with its Norman architecture, and famous frieze, designed by Lockyard Kipling, Rudyard's father, into which my mother, without warning, vanished while my father sighed, wry, resigned, "An overpowering desire has seized her." Carpe Diem. Quickly. I got him to let me buy books, second-hand, putative classics I had not yet ticked off the long lists at the back of those I had read (first oppressions of the heavy weight of unread literature!) while he, free, bought the penknives he loved, with a Ripleyesque array of ingenious, just-in-case-I'm-marooned attachments; and inventive kitchen gadgets that never worked for long, and similarly doomed coasters with henpecked husband lamentations, *My wife is my life, my life is my wife. What a wife! What a life!*

As December unraveled, scruffy neighborhood boys gathered at street corners, singing *Christmas is coming; the geese are getting fat; please put a penny in the old man's hat* as they fanned a twiggy, wavering fire. Pointing at their scarecrow in his faded shirt, they jauntily asked, "A penny for the old guy?" Guy Fawkes, I suppose, morphed into the old guy, the old year.

Eat, visit, shop, explore. Days devoted to pleasure reveal their hollow core sooner than days of work. Can pleasure possibly pall? By mid-December, it did.

"Now, let's go to Mangalore and see Ma," my father said with the defiant, tremulous firmness he rarely mustered. When he did however, he was – almost – unassailable.

"*Mangalore!*" said my mother. She was "a Bombayite," proud of her citizenship in the metropolis. "*Never!* I am never going to *set foot* in Mangalore again. *Petit pays, petite gens.* Everyone thought the Japanese were behind the Port Dock Explosion of 1942" and so, like Blitzed London children, the Bombayites who could evacuate did so. No Narnia though. "When we cried in Mangalore and said we missed our Mummy, those Konkani speaking girls asked, 'And do you miss your Puppy?'"

"I am a *persona non grata* in Mangalore," my mother said, with a pleased, twisted smile. The Latin, or...? The ill-fated visit. Twenty years ago. My soft-spoken father, Noel, the longed-for first-born son after "a plague of girls," five pretty maids all in a row, had returned after eight years in England, with a professional degree: F.C.A., Fellow of the Institute of Chartered Accountants, England and Wales; an English accent; rumored romances, never confirmed, never denied; urbanity; high culture – Malcom Sargent's *Messiah* at the Royal Albert Hall! Laurence Olivier as Lear at the Old Vic! Joyce, Woolf, Camus, Gide! and variegated experience: fruit-picking vacations in Europe; young communist camps in Poland; cricket matches at Lords after which, he said, triumphant West Indians raced onto the field, and tossed their cricket bats in the air, singing, "Crick-et, lubberly crick-et." As far as his mother, grandmother, and sisters were concerned, any bride must necessarily fall short of his glory. My mother, dissenting, never returned to Mangalore, nor met her mother or sisters-in-law again, winning the Pyrrhic battles between mother- and daughter-in-law scripted by centuries of Indian tradition by ignoring as thoroughly as she was ignored, a simple, overlooked strategy (if you can get away with it)!

"Pa, I'm going with you," I said desperately.

"No. *No!*" my mother said, equally desperately. "Your hair will look like the wild woman of Borneo's. You'll wear jeans in which your thighs look like the rocks of Gibraltar. You'll blab family secrets. They'll ask "Who do you like more, your mummy or your daddy?' and you will say my father, and they'll say why, and pump, and pump, and you are such a donk…"

"I'm *not* a donk."

"If the cap fits, wear it," she sang out gleefully.

"Oh, let her come," my father said. "Or you two will fight all the time. Next-door cornered me within a day and said, 'I *hear* Anita's back.'"

"Well, she'll be Mary, Mary, quite contrary in Mangalore too. She'll say, 'I'm called the naughtiest girl in school.' And they'll say why, and she's such a donk, she'll *explain – proudly –* and there'll be a new series of stories, and…" my mother squawked.

To Mangalore we went.

2 | The Winters of the Matriarchs

Bombay to Mangalore. "Pa, Pa, look," black-faced langur monkeys, a slender lori. Sliding backwards in time through the ancient hilly rain forests, luna-moth-green valleys and hairpin beds of the Western Ghats.

We took a "deluxe" cushiony bus, air-conditioned, but, alas, Emerson's crack, Murphy's rub, every air-conditioned coach was also a "video coach." By day, by night. So while my father and I played loud determined games of "Twenty Questions," or "Animal, Vegetable, Mineral, Thing," widows wailed, abandoned women in white wandered, listlessly singing *mera jeevan gora kagaj,* "my life is a blank page," and coquetteish brilliantly clad nymphs, nasal sopranos, darted around trees fleeing from shaggy satyrs called Amitabh or Rishi – all the while singing.

My father quizzed me, in the style of BBC's Mastermind, all the rage: "Who painted "The Persistence of Memory?'" "Salvador Dali." "What is Bob Dylan's real name?" "Robert Zuckerman. He called himself Dylan in homage to Dylan Thomas," I added gratuitously. "Whose epitaph was *Here he lies where he longed to be; Home is the sailor, home from the sea, And the hunter home from the hill?*" Later, in an embarrassing epiphany, I suspected my father asked facts he suspected I knew. Then we practiced debating, my father setting me topics like those in school – "Which is better, newspapers or television?" "An arranged marriage is better than a love marriage," and five minutes to scribble an introduction, body, and conclusion, and then, hoping he'd notice the brilliant bits, over the raucous screen, I declaimed my speech.

Every few hours, the bus pulled into a wayside restaurant, undoubtedly pre-arranged, pre-bribed. And since my father spent in a hay-making, mouse-playing way in my mother's absence, I ordered ecstatically: puri pallya, round deep-fried flatbreads with spinach; masala dosas, crisp golden, stretching far beyond the plate, stuffed with yellow oniony potatoes and oozing mustard seeds; and kulfi falooda, almond ice cream floating with red jelly, and vermicelli in a rose-syrupy pink milkshake – until even the waiter suggested desisting. My father ordered coffee. The waiter, beaming, cooled the coffee by letting the fragrant steaming ribbon cascade from one stainless tumbler to another three feet below; not a drop was spilled. "Coffee-by-the-yard," my father explained, sotto voce. "Order something, Pa!" My father grinned, "I'll see what you leave, *then* I'll order." "Oh, *I'm* ravenous!" I gourmandized. Ten minutes later: "I'm *full!*" Satiety hurt. "Eat some more." "I just can't," and my father emptied the almost full dishes, saying as I knew he would, "*Wasting!* When I was a student in England during the War, there were billboards everywhere showing a plate of half-eaten food. The caption said: 'If you didn't want it, why did you take it?'" At least I was spared the usual sour cliché: "her eyes are bigger than her stomach."

Then I was sent to the bathroom, and returned stricken. "Pa, there were lumps of shit in the squat toilet. I felt like throwing up." "Okay," he said, "Hurry. We'll find bushes." We walked into the scrub by the side of the road with him on guard duty. "You see the advantages of being a man!" he grumbled, as I again squealed, "Pa, is anyone coming?" "I can pee standing up, with my back to the road, and no one will guess what I'm doing." As if I needed convincing! "The poor parents!" my father'd say when he heard of the birth of a girl. "Girls are a terrible thing. A terrible responsibility." "If bandits come up to you and say, 'Your money or your life,' always say, 'Take my money,'" he'd instruct. "Huh! And what would you say, Pa?" "Take my wife," he grinned.

A rambunctious medical student from Manipal Medical College distributed sugarcane he'd snatched through the bus window from lumbering bullock carts. I crunched the nectary stalks with delight which faded when my father said the load would be weighed at the journey's end, and the driver, who sat oblivious, switching the magnificent white beasts, would be fined for the short. The student organized the English-speaking passengers into Canterbury riddle-askers, joke-tellers. "Knock, knock." "Who's there?" "Amos." "Amos Who?" "Amos Quito."

"A Sardarjee went to Bombay craning his neck at skyscrapers. A city slicker says, 'That's *my* building. Give me a rupee for every storey you looked at.' The Sardarjee later says slyly, 'I gave him fifteen rupees, but *actually* – I looked at *the whole building.*'" Just before the bus left Maharashtra, policemen, rifles in their holster, boarded it, searching luggage. Our heart stopped. The Scotch. Illegally procured as gifts through an army friend (the army had access to choice and subsidized liquor) but contraband in Maharastra: "Dry" – perennial, laudable, doomed social experiment. A drunk man yelled at the officials, who yanked him off the bus. Suddenly sober, he realized he had been arrested, and wept and pleaded with them, touching their feet. "They'll take every paise he has," my father said. "What a terrible thing it is to be drunk."

* * *

The Angelus bells pealed in peace as, at dawn, we entered Mangalore, our God-haunted ancestral town – a holy town, nuns and priests as common on the streets as secular people, like statue-studded ancient Athens in whose streets, it was said, one was as likely to encounter a God as a man. The nunnery and the seminary were traditional refuges for unmarried women of good family, or intellectual men who dreaded "settling down," and the arid busyness of the world of business. Two thousand nuns, and a thousand priests in Mangalore: a proud statistic we often heard, hence the frequent laughter of liturgical bells.

Mangalore resembled a tropical English village, as unlikely as a Pre-Raphaelite landscape that never was on sea or land: moist, leaf-green, very-green everywhere, as if it has just rained, dew seeping through emerald moss on the contorted roots of mango trees, and dripping from creepers and purple orchids. I have encountered other villages like Mangalore – in Costa Rica, for instance – with a sense of déjà vu, perhaps anticipating the day when all rivers will rush into one river, and all gardens merge into one garden, and the name of that garden shall be Eden.

The tang of the sea was in the air. Steep, shady lanes wound between rambling houses surrounded by gardens dense with palm and jackfruit trees, hibiscus and bougainvillea. Fruit-heavy branches lolled over garden walls, shedding roadside litter: guavas, avocados, mangoes. Fallen custard apples cracked open, spilling their sweet, white, seedy flesh.

The mossy old manses with their roofs of tunnel-shaped ochre tiles provided a sober counterpoint to the emigrant houses on the outskirts in Disneyland pink, turquoise, yellow and purple, extravagant monstrosities often, an irresistible exhibition of the fruits of lonely tropical toil, built – in the grand tradition of returnee housing, whether in Victorian England or colonial Spain – for their families by the thousands of Mangalorean working in the Persian Gulf. "Gulf money," one said wryly, passing them.

* * *

In a little black and yellow auto-rickshaw, or "bone-shaker," we rattled to "Palm Grove," my grandmother's house, which was secluded in a dark mosquitoey compound sheltered by high walls, and surrounded by swishing palm trees up which Billavas shimmied, small sickles around their waists, to retrieve the coconuts she sold them. They parked their bikes in the town's shady nooks, roped cascades of green, smooth-skinned coconuts dangling from the handlebars and back-carriers. A swipe of a machete and a straw; they sold passersby the cool, sweet coconut juice, the country's purest drink, safer even than water. Another swipe, and they returned the split coconut with a chip of its own husk to spoon up the delicate, creamy coconut meat. "Let nothing be wasted."

Then onto the long, shady verandah of Palm Grove, dark and cavernous, its high ceilings and stone floors keeping it cool as a morgue. Its red tiles, like those of many old houses in town, said Mssrs. Joseph Lobo and Son, the factory of Granny's father who left it to his naïve, sweet young third wife and widow, my great-grandmother Julianna. Julianna, baffled, sold it to her nephew for "a song" – the factory *and* the goodwill, as her son Norman discovered when he tried to establish a tile company with the family name. "The goodwill? Yes, I signed that. He said that meant I had no bad feelings." When Julianna's debts to my grandfather Piedade grew beyond hope of repayment, she signed over Palm Grove to her son-in-law. So Norman did not even inherit the ancestral home. Sad, guilty about this, my grandmother invited her younger brother to stay with her in his straitened old age, obviously deriving great comfort from her end being so close to her beginning.

Wiry, ectomorphic Norman was nimble, spry, Old Father William, a familiar sight around Mangalore, as he hopped on and off buses almost until his death at 102. A brusque old man with a savage wit. "How obsequious they were; now, when we pass the paddy fields, they show us their bums," – he rudely demonstrated – talking of land Granny had lost to her tenant farmers under India's socialist land-to-the-tillers legislation intended to crush the power of the *zamindars*, feudal landowners, who kept peasants in generational virtual serfdom. (A trivial unsinister debt at absurdly high interest to be paid off by unpaid labor, which meant further borrowing, further labor, a viciously circular debt, inherited by one's children and grandchildren, that two generations later goes *up*; there are fifteen million bonded child laborers in India.) Land ceiling, an excellent idea (my grandmother in Bombay gained a flat through an urban variety of such legislation) though the real feudal landowners, the unscrupulous and bullies with their hired thugs, retained their land through fraud and chicanery. I remember my classmate, Vanita, pulled out of class to doll up in a saree, makeup and bun of false hair, and, assisted by her own portliness, be presented in court as Mrs. Sabhrawal, independent farmer, thus evading the fifty acre per family land ceiling). Meanwhile the decent, the honorable, the clueless – the cartoonist, R.K. Lakshman's Common Man, unversed in the second language of the law – lost their land.

I dashed towards the dog on the verandah who strained towards me, snarling, steel chain taut, teeth bared. I boasted that I could gentle even savage Cave Canem watch dogs, talking to them at a distance, going ever closer, my outstretched hand just out of biting range, talking, talking, until their eyes hinted I could stroke them. But – can any crime be uglier than mutating the natural sweetness of an animal or a child? – Tibby had deliberately been brutalized.

And now memory cowers, as at the knowledge of a impending burn, and the memoirist's task is at its most whyish. In the lazy afternoons, Norman, siesta-rested, took his walking stick to methodically, savagely, beat the cowering dog who, with high broken-hearted yelps of desperation, helplessly bent his head, screwing his eyes shut in terror, as if blindness might shield him from pain. At any moment, the dog could have swerved and bitten the man, but did not; humane, brutish, imprecise adjectives. I rushed out, near hysteria; my father held me back, muttering, "It *is* his dog." "*Why?*" I asked the terrifying old man. Norman stalked off, glaring, mumbling. To render the dog furious, ferocious, so that, when unchained at night to prowl the grounds, he would instantly bite a burglar – following his new-grafted instincts.

* * *

We walked through the dark living room with its de rigueur shrine on a crocheted tablecloth: a pious assemblage of souvenirs from other people's trips to Rome, Lourdes, Fatima or our native Velankanni – cloudy bottles of holy water, silver cameo triptychs of the Holy Family, mortuary cards, "holy pictures." The "Sacred Heart" smiled, revealing his thorn-pierced heart. Rainbow lights twinkled around a blue-sashed haloed Virgin who, cupped in one's hands, glowed, eerie luminous phosphorous in the conjured darkness. The red glow of a Martian flame-shaped bulb bathed rosaries with gold and silver beads, and lingering figurines from the crib such as the recumbent Infant Jesus of Prague who kicked his silver legs in baby glee. "Everyday should be Christmas," went a popular sermon. Indeed!

The most frequent spiritual experience of my Catholic childhood was not the numinous – when the veil parts, and you glimpse the elegance of the Grandmaster, and time stands still while you are wracked by joy. That came, but later. My most common emotion was boredom – continuous mental calculations: the ratio of Hail Marys said to Hail Marys left. Of the Mass said to the Mass unsaid. In fractions, in decimals.

As I walked through Palm Grove, Norman growled from rooms away. "Anita, don't drag your feet." "What a disgrace, him having to scold you so often," my mother said later. "Why do you drag your feet?"

I dragged them to evening prayers at the family altar, squirmy phrase. Each evening, as darkness fell, Norman knelt on the cold stone floor to lead us in the rosary, his head tilted backwards to gaze at the Virgin, his arms outstretched like the crucified Christ (a quite unnecessary, unprescribed piety; wherever did he get the idea from?) outstretched rigidly, as sixty-six slow rosary beads dripped through his fingers, Credo, Pater Noster, Ave Maria, Gloria. "Hail Mary, full of grace," he proclaimed with brisk gusto and hints of admonishment: "See me, so old; see my reverence. *And yours?*" Or so I read the language of his body, as he trawled us through the rosary, present purgatory to abbreviate a future one. My father knelt, which he never did at home, unwilling to be shamed by his uncle's piety, or perhaps because he expected it was expected. A frown and downward tilt of his head suggested that I do likewise, which I did not, the embarrassment of conforming to this atypical sanctimoniousness being roughly equal to the embarrassment of refusing to.

"Holy Mary," my father muttered, frowning grimly as he did under scrutinizing eyes, as he did whenever I was in the vicinity of a nun, or a smiling gossip. And so it went on, sempiternal, Chinese water torture. Mosquitoes buzzed in the darkness; I wanted to itch. I wanted to bay. Though my grandmother, Josephine, sat primly in her rocking chair, studying her rosary beads, serious and contemplative as a Van Gogh woman, I wondered if she was enduring it as much as my father was, as much as I was, this flamboyant fervency imposed on us by Norman.

In the gathering darkness of the compound, dhoti-clad men, respectful of Norman's communion with the Almighty, waited. They watched the gaunt man kneel, cruciform, his El Greco face taut. "*Arre Baap*. He must be ninety."

How bland would pastures be without baa-baa black sheep, and boring cupboards without their skeleton.

"Someone." Isn't everyone someone? Apparently not. And so the toxic small town quest to be one of the "everybody who is anybody."

An in, an in; he said he had an in. Everyone's secret fear: that this is *exactly* how the world works, always an inner circle inner-er than your own; the kingdom, the power and the glory transmitted through loops closed to you. Mention my name, people say airily, perpetuating this impression, gaining free advertising. Norman knew someone who could swiftly get them passports, visas, jobs in the Gulf, literally Mecca to those who, though scornfully treated by arrogant Arabs, returned in airplanes uncomfortably overfull with food processors, color televisions and VCR's, having put money in their purse for neon houses, their children's education, and their own old age. "But hurry, hurry," his friend had only twenty-one openings.

"Hurry," should be spelled pause – as the once-burned learn. Shimmering hope. Documents signed without reading, a frenzy of borrowing, and other no-nos as they glimpse this beautiful shore on which one will be rich, and one will be glorious. Of course.

He got his twenty-one. Who daily, weekly, waited outside the columned porticoes of Palm Grove for news of their emigration. His mind filled with holy harmonies – *Father, forgive them*, he goes out to meet them, radiant, reproachful, a Lord of the manor to recalcitrant serfs. "O ye of little faith." Tomorrow and tomorrow and tomorrow. They wait, clutching hope. And who would suspect that octogenarian, gilded by his lengthy prayers, his silver hair, and his "good family," who in bank, boardroom, or monastery, serving God or serving mammon, rose to the top through nature and nurture – their dominant spiritual gene (a genetic trait, I suspect) and "the three I's: intelligence, integrity and industry," Mangalorean virtues, the community told itself complacently.

I wouldn't have suspected Norman. Neither did they, as they handed over borrowed money. The days became months, interest inexorably compounding, compounding. The would-be émigrés suspect; are smooth-talked, white-haired, blue-blooded out of their suspicions – furiously suspect – know. They visited his niece Eunice, a well-known plantation-owner, weeping: "How can God let this happen to us?" And, "What a disgrace," my Aunt Eunice said with widened eyes. "One of them committed *suicide*." A clerk in the electricity board who had handed over the small dowry garnered during a quarter century of penny-saved-penny-gained, scrimping, shaving, saving, short-shrift thrift begun with the birth of his five daughters. How replace the nest-egg he'd gathered, painful paise by paise? How face beginning again? His body swung metronomically from a ceiling fan. Then, a copycat suicide. His nephews confront Norman. "What money?" he asks, the injured, sinned-against, his role played so long that he forgot it was a role. (The bare-faced liar, the red-handed thief are as insulted by accusation as the lily-handed.)

Norman warns against tormenting him because God has been for him, visiting strange calamities on past persecutors. But ultimately: "I don't have it." He didn't – still the simple rainment, starched white cotton shirt and pants; he still skipped off and on buses; ate abstemiously at his sister's table. But where *was* the money? Good cop, bad cop, cajoling, threats. Private detectives. My very own Agatha Christie. I pumped, overheard, circuitously questioned, sat still as the proverbial owl: "The more he listened the more he knew, and oh, how wise that little owl grew." He had donated the money to the local cloistered nuns whose prayers, behind high walls, rose like incense as they ceaselessly interceded for the sins of the world.

To the nuns. "A fool and his money are soon parted," my father lamented ruefully when he spotted money in my purse (as inevitably as graffiti provoked the reflection, "The names of fools, like their faces, are often seen in public places.") The nuns were not fools. "But how do you know the money he gave us was *that* money? And anyway, we have spent it." Good cop, bad cop, cajoling, threats, to retrieve blood-money from the treasury. When I left the country, Norman, then ninety-two, was, with Barnum Bailey inventiveness, blood-sucking fresh suckers.

* * *

She sat in the sunlight streaming through the dining room window, a woman thinking; a study in chiaroscuro with her dark sarees and her fair-skinned, fine-featured, sunken face, her brother Norman invariably with her, the two old people remarkably alike, both inheriting their pale skin and pendulous ears from their Portuguese grandmother who left Granny but one, odd, tangible legacy – a chamber pot brought from Portugal with her name painted on it, *Donna Henrietta Maria Henderiquez.*

As she heard me drag my feet, Granny called from the dim dining room where she sat all day, a frail wraith, her voice soft, and tremulous with age, "Anita, come here; talk to me," – uninvited-fairy incantation, petrifaction. I slouched into the dining room. Pale and stern, she pointed, "Sit there. Talk to me." *Say something! What to say?* My mind froze. *The sedge is wither'd from the lake, and no birds sing.* "Tell me about your boarding school," she said. What about my boarding school? I could think of nothing about my boarding school. I sat there, rigor mortis on mind and tongue. After a decent but interminable interval, I escaped. The air on the verandah felt bright and free. My heart winged. "Pa, let's play Scrabble. Let's play Monopoly," I panted, diving into the games with ferocious, self-forgetting capitalistic passion. "Noel spends his visit to me playing Monopoly with Anita," his mother said.

My father said: "What do you mean you don't know what to say? An intelligent person should be able to have an interesting conversation with almost anyone. If all else fails, ask questions."

* * *

What is your earliest memory, Granny?

Standing in a mulberry field, overhearing a passerby say, "What a *beautiful* child!" "And that is how I knew I was beautiful." The Fall, and so, celestial taxation – each blessing: beauty, wealth, great talent conceals curse and hassle in its cracks (as curses reveal a silver thread of blessing). In an unabashedly fair-is-beautiful culture, Granny was married at seventeen to a man twice her age, as dark as she was "fair," my grandfather, Dr. Piedade Felician Mathias, a self-made Icarian surgeon who, through the combined effort of his entire family – and his own brilliance, sweat, resolve – went to medical school. During an uppity teenage phase of ours, my father scolded, "Now, now, don't get too snobbish. You don't know my father's family. One of them (the one who put Piedade through medical school incidentally) was a tonga-wallah." He gleefully claimed kinship with the butcher, an apocryphal one we hoped, the baker, the candlestick-maker, while we cried in only partially exaggerated distress, "Oh *Pa, stoooop*."

Did you like your husband, Granny? I asked, with curiosity which skirted rudeness, as her simplicity skirted senility. "I never liked him," she said, incredibly. "He had a very bad temper. I was always afraid of him," an almost sacrilegious statement in India. The professed religions of India are deeply, stubbornly, divisive, not so its unvoiced, axiomatic ones: the reverence of wealth and success, the imperatives of hospitality and generosity, and the benevolent religion of family which dictates, in one's discourse, at least, an affectionate sentimentality towards your blood relatives, a pretence that, of course, they were perfect and, of course, you loved them.

Where did he work?

(In the days when "the first" was offensively qualified by Indian) he was the first Indian Assistant Surgeon General in Madras, where he was also the first Indian Superintendent and Professor of Surgery of the Stanley Medical College (which still has a Dr. P.F. Mathias ward). He'd capture my father for company during his long days on the Madras docks where he vetted interminable lines of indentured laborers who, out of desperate poverty and familial love, left India for British colonies, Trinidad, Singapore, Malaya, Burma, Ceylon, Uganda, Kenya – scenes, decades later, of anti-Indian riots, unknowing sowing the vineyard of the grapes of wrath. The physicals were, perforce, perfunctory: Rasping, rattly lungs: TB; pull down the lower eyelid, too pale, too anemic; open your mouth, good teeth, good general health. Vice-versa. A scribe followed. A minute a man.

He received two imperial decorations, the Kaiser-i-Hind medal in 1921, and, at the Imperial Durbar in 1929, the O.B.E. Lolling in the verandah, I'd read his O.B.E. citation mechanically, dreamily, "We George Fifth, King Emperor of Great Britain, North Ireland, and the British Dominions beyond the Seas, Defender of the Faith, to our Trusty and Well-beloved Piedade Felician Mathias, Greetings…" Or something to that effect. On the day before he left to the Imperial Durbar, he froze. How exactly does one tie a tie? And so, on the day before his day of exaltation, he humbly went to ask his Portuguese Parish priest.

In whom he had selective faith. My father pointed out the abandoned "haunted" house of his friend and fellow altar-boy Noel Davis, whose sister Jessie was "possessed." He'd whisper between the Kyrie and the Sanctus, "Noel, does this happen in your house? It's terrible! At night, winds blow though our house. Stones fall. Little chalices rain down." When the Portuguese Parish priest went to exorcize Jessie, my grandfather snorted, "*He* can't cast out demons. He's too fat. You have to be able to *fast* to do that."

What else do you remember?

After he successfully operated on a Brother of Saint Gabriel, the Order which ran Montfort, my father's boarding school, the Superior visited him: "Oh, Dr. Mathias, he was invaluable to the Order; how can we thank you? You saved his life." Piedade replied in the Latin of a thousand masses, *Non nobis Domine, non nobis, sed nomini tuo da gloriam*; "Not to us, O Lord, not to us; but to Thy name give the glory," Psalm 115.

And he bled Scripture. A servant girl, recommended by the said Parish Priest, ran away with the gold jewelry which Granny (whose carelessness sounds ruefully familiar) had left on her dressing table, and which represented Piedade's life savings, gold being a "safe" investment, certain to appreciate as long as men mistake wives for trophies and women are vain. (In good times, your wife bedecks herself to general feminine envy and nagging. In desert times – let's not think about that.) Tell the priest, track her down? Siphon time from today's work in a wild gold chase? Dr. Mathias shrugged sadly, quoting Job, *The Lord gives, the Lord takes away; blessed be the name of the Lord*, and went back to work, slowly replacing the trove.

Wisdom and prudence became additional themes of his life, as were faith, hard work, success in his career *and* financially. He invested in land, which can only be lost in crooked courts, buying property with prescient shrewdness (one of those surprisingly uncommon people who could translate high IQ into hard cash) in the center of Mangalore, and in Cubbon Road, the posh heart of Bangalore, near both the Residency, now Raj Bhavan, the Governor's mansion; and today's granite Vidhana Soudha, State Legislature, land that, like gold, was unlikely to depreciate, whatever the fate of the Bank of England. He died at fifty-eight, intestate, leaving sufficient money for Josephine, a widow for fifty-three years; for college educations for his daughters (Jessie became one of community's earliest "lady doctors") as well as his sons; dowries for the girls; start-up funds for the boys; farmland, rental properties, and sixty years of wrangling over them.

He worked God, and God, with mercy and amusement, allowed Himself to be worked. When his private practice dropped, he'd say, aggrieved, accusatory, "Josephine are you giving? Give. You are not giving; that is why I am not getting." She did; people got sick; he bought land, houses, including her mother's.

Imprinting. As a widow, on the first Monday of the month, Granny had her chair carried out to her palm grove, where – word spreading on the wings of the wind – waited the blind, the halt, the merely poor. To each: a five rupee note, a smile. "Stop this," remonstrated the son and grandson who had taken her in hand, agonized, as she extricated the staple from yet another wad of fresh fivers: "To you, and you, and you." "If you *have* to give money away, give it to the parish priest. He'll know the truly needy cases." "No, no!" she said. "He'll just give it to his own people. I'd rather give it to people *I* know." "How do you know these people are needy?" they asked. "If they weren't, why would they come?" she retorted with sublime simplicity – and probably correctly.

Morris, the richest of her sons, indulgently sent her, each month, a few hundred rupees – to give away. "Give, Ma, give," he laughed, remembering his father's powerful, paradoxical economy. "The more you give, the more we get." She gave the gourmet cheeses and chocolates (her favorite foods) that Morris sent her from Singapore to her live-in servant Leela's fair, pretty little girl with whom in her old age, she – who had so coveted boys – fell in love. "The baby needs it more than I do," she said, when her carers protested: "They probably haven't even acquired the taste for them." And not just cholesterol. Realizing that sweet-natured Leela and that adorable toddler would be homeless after her death, reduced to rolling beedis all day (ubiquitous cheap microcigars, "the poor man's cigarette"; Mangalore Ganesh is India's largest brand) she promised them her ancestral house, Palm Grove. *Non compos mentis*, law suit, some daughters muttered darkly, suspecting she would leave her property to her bossiest son – as she did. If they'd heard of this! Leela stayed on at Palm Grove after Granny's death, maintaining, despite the flourished will, "She *gave* me the house." Threats, cajoling, reluctant refusals to police and goondas who appeared: "You want her out; leave it to us. It will be ..." until the house was sold, the ayah still in it, lured out with some of the proceeds, "sharing the inheritance as one of the brothers."

Did you want so many children, Granny? I asked, skidding on the slippery slope of personal questions. "No," she said simply, Topsy-like. "I never wanted so many. I just had them." A rare admission, particularly in a culture of gushing and glorying over children, and guilt-inducing "missing" them.

Celestial economics, celestial medicine. In the days when amniocentesis must have sounded like a wish-fulfillment fantasy, my grandfather selected gender by prayer. At first, unsuccessfully. Eunice, Minnie, Jessie, Dora, Priscilla, five unwanted maids all in a row, each pregnancy commencing with "*Pray. Pray for a boy,*" and bitterly culminating with "*Another girl! That's because you did not pray hard enough,*" and so they did, desperately, and then:

eight pretty boys all in a row, the Mangalorean gold standard of blessing.

Fourteen children, pepper and salt, some "fair" like their mother ("I was pulled over for speeding in the States, and the cop wrote Race: White"); others, dark-skinned, and – irritatingly unpolitically correctly – the lighter-skinned, my father among them, were mild, phlegmatic, scholarly, urbane, while, generally, the darker tended to be pugnacious, aggressive, tilting at the windmills of the business world, a little frightening.

Piedade and Josephine, at great expense, sent their children to the Montfort School in Yercaud, run by Belgian Brothers, where they received a classical education: Latin, French, Shakespeare, poetry; the alumni became doctors, lawyers, judges, senior civil servants, especially after Independence. The parents' intention: an alchemical transmutation into something like Macaulay's conceited conceit of the brown-skinned gentlemen; *a class of persons, Indian in blood and color, but English in taste, in opinions, in morals, and in intellect.* Again: initial disappointment. Josephine described her sons in her much-threatened, then much-quoted letter to the Brothers. "They blow in their coffee; they pour it into their saucers; they take a mile on each side of them. They are boors."

The boors got the haircuts they deserved. Josephine, once a month, lined her fourteen pretty children all in a row, placed a mixing bowl on their heads, and cut their hair like a Gordian knot, shearing all erring curls. My father, her first-born son, faced a different Scylla: His mother could not bear to cut his Absalom ringlets, which curled below his shoulders, stroked by the old, pulled by the young. And so, in the kind of irony which must make God smile, the coveted boy looked girlish. His sisters recited their mother's litany, with an undercurrent of bitterness beneath the mirth: "Eunice, Minnie, comb Noel's hair; Eunice, Minnie, put on Noel's shoes." Even his forbidding father pampered him, buying him a pony called Paddy, and a donkey called Ned.

From her still point in front of the sunny dining room window, where she gazed at the sun-bright backyard pond (near which her three year old son, Charlie, had lain mesmerized, watching the lotus bloom, and the bright carp flash, and where his drowned body was found, floating limp among the flowers) Granny cooked – in a manner of speaking. My mother, as a young bride experimenting with the recommended below-the-belt routes to a man's heart, asked for the recipes my father wisted over. "Golden Syrup on toast," he longed. "Treacle on toast." "How do you make Golden Syrup?" she enquired. And where in India does one find a treacle well? Neither love nor money could conjure up Golden syrup or treacle; India then sensibly banned imports of consumer goods to nurture its nascent industries (which sadly under iniquitous World Trade Organization rules it can no longer do, leading to the suicide of farmers who cannot afford royalties to Ricetec in America when they plant the newly patented Basmati.) "Golden Syrup? I boiled sugar in water, and fed it to those bounders when they returned ravenous from boarding school," Granny replied. "I called it Golden Syrup, and they were happy." Syrup rendered golden by boyhood's unappeasable hunger, my father's mythopoeic memory, and the magic of language! She would not be drawn into more talk of recipes. "I cook by instinct," she said, a statement my mother mimicked in a hoity-toity, eyebrows-raised voice. And so she did, by instinct, memory, and remote control, summoning the cook, describing a Platonic curry, prescribing a recipe. The cook brought her a taste in a small stainless steel dish. "More salt, more coriander, a little grated coconut, let it thicken for another, oh…seven minutes" until imagination became curry, and appeared before us, and we tasted its glory.

In her household, one slid backwards in time. The water from the backyard well looked yellow, and tasted stale, contradicting the properties of water I'd learnt in chemistry: colorless, odorless, tasteless. Baths were a more fraught enterprise than switching on a geyser at home where the only admonition was "Don't let it overheat, or it will explode. So-and-so *died* when their geyser exploded." Here, double, double toil and trouble; fire burn, and cauldron bubble; you told Granny, who told the servant, who lit the nest of firewood beneath the smoldering copper cauldron, which fumed and hissed as you dipped your bronze urn, a *chembu* into it, as gingerly (particularly during power cuts) as if that smoke-blackened bathing room were Bluebeard's den, careful not to topple the cauldron, or blister your hands on its sides. "The cauldron tipped on R. Terrible scarring. Her parents will have to pay for plastic surgery, or she'll never get married."

The coffee at breakfast was rich-sweet with golden lumps of jaggery or gur, unrefined sugar, eschewed by my parents because of the occasional embedded straw or suspect pellets acquired from the dirt floor of country barns on which it had congealed. (My dreams of wealth and adulthood included all the gur I cared to eat). And with the coffee, *Kube*, cockles in a coconut and jaggery curry. Eating seashells, extricating elusive sea-worms from the lovely homes they hefted around – a moralist's object lesson on the misery of possessions – was more trouble than it was worth, much like eating the marrow of mutton bones, "the best part," the old ladies said, as they passed around their hairpins.

What are you reading, Granny?

For she always was: a biography of Francis Xavier, perhaps, and each week, cover to cover, the international edition of *Time* magazine which Morris sent her, her opinions on world politics incisive, decisive, shared as freely as her gnomic social maxims. "Don't get a Ph.D. Nobody marries a woman better educated than they are. If you get a Ph. D., who will you find to marry you?" or "Family is more important than the boy. Don't look at the boy so much as the family," or, oddly, exactly what Mother Teresa told me a decade later, "You *can't* remain single; get married or become a nun."

Once, as Granny sat reading – one of my mother's most reproachful "your mother" reproaches – Sister Columba, my mother's beloved eightyish great-aunt, affectionate, gentle, completely sweet, rattled across Mangalore in an uncomfortable "bone-shaker" to see us. The tiny nun walked up the verandah stairs to my grandmother, whose house it, after all, was, arms outstretched, smiling with every evidence of delight, chirping in the over-accentuated, effusive, mellifluous Mangalorean style, in the high-pitched cooing intonations of socialese the world over, "Jose – phine, It's An – niie. Do you remember me? We were classmates." They had not met for seventy years.

My grandmother looked up, a shade contemptuously, "You've not come to see me. You've come to see Anita and Noel," turned on her heel, marched in. Sister Columba's small face puckered in hurt and bewilderment. She nervously clasped and unclasped her hands. When had she last encountered sheer rudeness? Perhaps never. "Poor thing," my mother said, reliving the scene, growing, each time, more upset.

Since successful men married the youngest, prettiest bedfellows they could find, prodigious bearers of children, nurses in old age, widowhood was an inevitability universally acknowledged. My great-grandmother, Julianna, who bore six children in her brief years as a wife, was a widow for seventy-three years; Granny – widowed in her forties, her fourteenth child a newborn – for fifty-three. The pants, the bacon, it made one tough. If Granny had ever tolerated foolishness, such foolishness had long been leached out. A rusty old spade was a spade, and – in a culture which valued courtesy, sweetness, graciousness, excellent traits in women – she, though gentle of face and voice, refused to call it a silver spoon or a golden rule.

When I fought with my mother, fierce-tongued and ferocious, my father shook his head. "I would never have *dared* to speak to my mother like that," he said. "If she gave me an order even today, I would obey her. One night she punished my brother, Michael at dinner by making him kneel on the dining table. When she came down to breakfast the next morning, having quite forgotten about Michael, there he was, asleep, swaying on his knees."

* * *

At last, Christmas. Open air Midnight Mass. *Gloria in Excelsius Deo* resounded thrillingly from thousands of silk-saried women, and smart-suit-and-tied men. Traditional post-midnight Mass sweet homemade wine, for adult and child alike. My father's sisters arrived the next day with potato chops and minced beef "cutlets," croquettes, freshly prepared by their cooks for their mother. And small gifts for me. "She prayed for good Christmas presents all last night," my father laughed, while I hissed "*Pa*," as embarrassed as his richest sister, who gave me a single chocolate bar, a serendipitously gold-foil-wrapped Five Star with a pink ribbon tied around it. I innocently and sententiously mused a little later, recycling a just-heard epigram, "The world is divided into givers and takers." "I'm a giver," she said swiftly. Afterwards, my father chuckled, "Fitzgerald said, 'The rich are the rich because they spend less money.'"

A sacrosanct tradition probably borrowed from the Portuguese: To visit all one's friends and family in the twelve days between Christmas and the Feast of the Epiphany on the sixth of January, The Visit of the Magi to Bethlehem, the official end of the season. Nuns first: my great-grandmother Alice Rebello's siblings, Sister Columba at the Apostolic Carmel, a mainly Mangalorean teaching order; Sister Marie Agnes at the Cloistered Carmel; and the eldest, Sister Marie Therese of the Little Sisters of the Poor, at whose growing decrepitude my father was, each year, appalled. "She looked terrible – wizened," he'd report. "Those nuns don't look after her. All her teeth have fallen out, and they haven't got her dentures. How can she eat meat?" His mother, and the old ladies who sat with her in the evenings, listened – with prurient avidity, the arena of competition shifted from beauty-spouse-wealth, to one's childrens' plummy college-spouse-career, to "the one who dies last wins" – and beneath the rapid-fire questions and veneer-thin concern with which the ancients enquire about detached retinas, open heart surgery, deafness, diabetes, aneurysms, you hear a note of *schadenfreude* (why doesn't English have a word for it?); pride – "I've escaped;" and fear – "for now."

Sister Marie Therese escorted us around the wards and grounds, Virgilianly, visitors from a sun-bright world, pointing out, thumb-nail sketching the inmates – old, sick, destitute or disabled. My expected smile felt as awkward as I did. And then, dreaded Pew, the blind man, the Sisters of Charity's living sermon. He sat on the floor in shorts, spindly legs crossed. "Sing, Joseph," they told him, "Sing." He obliged in a high-pitched, nasal, slightly cracked voice, the pupils of his eyes rolling, his head tilted at an unnatural angle: *When upon life's billows you are tempest-tossed,/ When you are discouraged, thinking all is lost,/ Count your blessings; count them one by one/ And it will surprise you what the good Lord has done./ Count...*

I knew what I was expected to think, and, slightly irritated, I thought it: "Look at this poor blind man counting his blessings, though he has so few. And how much more should I...?

And then, customary culmination: my father took out his checkbook. The Superior was summoned. Christmas-eve electricity. The nuns surrounded us, beaming at me; the benefaction had bestowed sudden swan-feathers, gilding, absolution.

"How much, Pa?" I asked on our way home. "Two hundred rupees." "Pa! *Two hundred rupees*. And Ma said I couldn't have those high-heeled mirror-worked, embroidered Rajasthani sandals." My sister's pair were her most treasured possession; as she came out of anesthesia after eye surgery at ten, her first words were, "Where are my sandals?" "Be quiet, Anita," he said. "You don't need high-heeled, mirror-worked, embroidered Rajasthani sandals. Didn't you hear Granny tell us how Grandpa gave money away *especially* when he needed it. Don't you read the Sermon on the Mount? It's a promise. 'Give and you shall receive, full measure, pressed down, flowing over.'" Measure for Measure. A law of life."

"Acting on that really takes faith," I thought. "Okay," I said, "Okay." Though I still wanted the high-heeled shoes.

My great-aunt Sister Mary Agnes was the (first Indian) prioress of the Cloistered Carmel Convent whose nuns, cloistered for life, bound by vows of silence, somehow knew much of what went on upstairs and downstairs and in my lady's chamber in all the houses of the town, from the least to the greatest. The town could, of course, pray for itself; professionals were inessential; however, the wise realized that the work of prayer was more exhausting, more wrenching, more exacting of faith, hope and love than mere work. So, supported by honey brought by worker bees to the heart of the heart of the hive, the nuns lived as birds, bees and lilies do, on faith, hope and love, a economy which works for those with the guts for it. And the town was unusually prosperous: many successful citizens, its families close-knit, generous with loans, jobs and shelter to their weaker members, so who knows? – those invisible bees probably did produce palpable sweetness.

They had prayed with and for my parents though their seven year struggle to conceive; through the birth of a son, that greatest blessing; through his death three days later; and my birth a year after that: "the child of their prayers." As tidings of my visit swished through silent corridors, a collage of brown-swathed faces formed around the grille. Sister Gabrielle, a jolly, fat French nun whose particular prayer project I was, corresponded with me in idiosyncratic Franglish for years. "Sister *pray*, I'm dieting. Again." "Yes, but *promenade*." In my soulful phases, I replied with soulful musings, which were the truth, nothing but the truth – I was God-fearing – but not, alas, the whole truth. I read her reply in flourishes and capitals to my father, "You are the Pearl of the Orient," then regretted that spot of showing off when he infuriatingly persistently dubbed me Pearly.

The Cloistered Carmel was the repository of the town's secrets and I, unworthily, satisfied my idle curiosity once I learnt the cryptology of the face: the quizzical glance, the faint ironic smile, the double-underlining of names and phrases, a language of intonation and implication common to religious people. "Pray for X; he really needs your prayers." And why, prithee? And when you bared your soul, if you could think the unthinkable: that you might not be more special and beloved than all the other sad, striving, desperate "Sister pray for me's," you might reluctantly make an inference. The portress alone had relatively untrammeled access to the outer world. (My great-aunt who joined the Cloistered Carmel in 1903, aged eighteen, left for the first time to attend a Convention of Cloistered Carmel Prioresses in 1954, riding in a car to the train, neither of which she'd seen before!) In my last visit before I left India, the portress, in a startling reversal, startled *me* with her whispered advice, "Never marry a foreigner; they are like dogs running after a hundred bitches" – the wild west of nunnish fantasy.

My grandmother Josephine's sister, Catherine, now Mother Ambrose, a Good Shepherd nun, had blood-boiling accounts of the indignities of colonial convents. The white nuns made the Indian nuns wear different habits, sit in a different section of the chapel, undertake the menial chores, the kitchen, the laundry, much like lay brothers in medieval monasteries. I think of *The Last Battle*, Lewis's final chilling Narnia novel, about the exploitation and suffering inflicted by those who claim to speak for Aslan, on the trusting ones who love Aslan, and so endure them for his dear sake.

* * *

My father's sister Eunice, grandest of the town's grand old ladies, was nicknamed the Grand-Duchess; (my grandmother was the Empress, and Aunt Minnie, the Duchess). Her face, a mask of hauteur, tight pursed lips, eyebrows and nostrils raised in habitual disdain, resembled a severe ruffed Old Master Renaissance Queen's, say, Velasquez's Empress Isabella at the Prado. The right numbers in marriage's lottery – and long habit gave her the manner of one to the manor born.

Her good fortune came, in its insidious way, with a catch: a familiar one – the Indian cliché, the villainous mother-in-law. The whisper: "The horror always lived with them. Eunice never had a proper married life." "That mother-in-law!" my grandmother had fretted when the proposal came. "Worry not," the matchmaker, Bella, reassured her. "She's a sickly old thing. She'll die any day now, and Eunice will have a happy married life." "The matchmaker died!" my father said. "Never count on anyone dying. Those on the verge of death linger there for a long time, coddling themselves, being coddled, while the apparently healthy drop dead in an instant."

From the egg of inherited coffee estates, Eunice's only son created gaggles of golden geese – canning and exporting the goodness of Arabian Ocean, crab, shrimp, lobster, oysters; buying factories, and eventually constructing a real estate empire: entire neighborhoods of apartment buildings becoming, probably, South India's largest real estate developer. When, in the universally acknowledged way of single men in possession of a good fortune, he married, Eunice insisted that the bride live with them in the ancestral house, scene of her old travails. But! "The woman who sleeps next to a man has his ear," Aunt Eunice said vindictively over her dining table lavish with lobsters and oysters (which I had for the first time at her house), crab curry, and duck molee in coconut gravy. The ancient, bitter battle of two women for a man's soul, the younger woman with her age-old biological weapons: youthful beauty, motherhood, and sexual attraction, antique welder of seismic power; the older lady with hers: tears, guilt, accusation, and the subliminal glue of primeval bonding and long obedience. But we have it on the highest authority that the meek (the daughters-in-law), will eventually, temporarily, inherit the earth. An often heard anecdote, true in spirit, at least. The evil mother-in-law serves herself and her son boiled white rice, giving the daughter-in-law the *kunji*, strained water. The mother and son look sickly, while the daughter-in-law perversely thrives, growing *thugda*, solid, and strong on the lees – full of the B-vitamins unwittingly boiled out.

Two queen bees? An impossibility. Usually, finally, comes the day of the new queen. Who swarmed. I listened, I listened; the world lay before me as various, as beautiful, as new as a longed-for, unread book, and I read it by the golden light of fiction, seeking one to one correspondences between books and life, life and books, seeing uncanny parallels between Maggie Tulliver's three aunts in *The Mill on the Floss*, the wealthy formidable Aunt Glegg, doleful Aunt Pullet, and quiet Aunt Deane and my own three aunts, while identifying with Maggie, passionate, harum-scarum, odd and square in a too small, too round duck pond.

Then to my funny, warm aunt Minnie and her husband, Laurie (one of those couples one suspects of a diet as convenient as the Sprats). Laurie, dark, simple, slim, always-smiling, was a shadowy presence quite eclipsed by his large, jocose wife; in memory he walks, always, a few steps behind her. Aunt Minnie had worn whale-bone corsets, a curiosity we gaped at, until she gave up dresses, and her battle with bulges. She now raised her massive arms and let her nieces and nephews jiggle her rolls of fat.

"Remember when you wore Minnie's dress and rung the front door bell?" Laurie asked. My father, who graduated from college in 1937 during the Great Depression, lodged with Minnie in Delhi, while working his first job, clerical, ill-paid – but a job.

And Minnie laughed, "And little Derek did not recognize him, and said, "Mummy, there's an old lady at the door, asking for you."

"And how wicked he was, Anita. When we slept on the verandah on hot summer evenings, he'd wait till poor Laurie fell asleep, then throw a wooden cotton reel at the fan."

"And Laurie would wake, jerking his arms and legs into the air, upended spider-like, and say, "*What's that? What's that?*" " My father grinned, a little embarrassed. "And I'd wait till he fell asleep, then do it again."

In a family in which post-name letters were a minimum requirement – my grandfather, an F.R.C.S., Fellow of the Royal College of Surgeons; my father, an FCA; Fellow of the Institute of Chartered Accountants, England and Wales; other siblings with an M.D. or Ph.D. – Minnie gaily presented her credentials, J.C.F., Junior Cambridge Failed. She had sobbed for her mother in boarding school until she was summoned home.

After Laurie died, Aunt Minnie became the lachrymose aunt, bursting into tears at the thought of Laurie, and she thought of him often. Bereavement: horrid cocktail of guilt, loneliness, and grief, perennial pain from a phantom limb. Then, archeology. "Poor Minnie, all the shocks of the family fell on her. She was the one who went in and discovered Daddy dead – just after he told her to call his lawyer to, at last, write his will. When your aunt Prissie – she was a student at Stanley Medical College – died of sunstroke while swimming, Minnie took the call," Aunt Eunice said. "When our sister Dora's – she had eyes like yours, Anita – stiletto heels got stuck in the tram tracks in Madras, and she was crushed to death, Minnie was with her."

My father's youngest sister, Juno, a school-teacher with a homely pleasant face, and salt-and-pepper hair straying from her "bun," lived in a little frond-swished cottage on the grounds of Palm Grove. She was a favorite among us twenty-seven first cousins – interestingly – for she, detached, self-sufficient, apparently did nothing to court our affections; her breezy will o' the wisp manner was like the genie curls and whirls from the round-the-clock cigarettes she smoked, and let us puff, so that, mostly, our first acrid, gagging encounter with nicotine was our last. She was, in fact, often preoccupied – with crossword puzzles which she solved obsessively, and with books into which she escaped, unable to sleep until she had read some Graham Greene, even when she returned at 3 a.m. from parties with her beautiful, popular daughter, Veronica.

Juno's approach to food was slapdash, her combinations bizarre – canned sardines and strawberry jam. Mackerel and condensed milk. "Mind your own business," she snapped with unusual acerbity when we commented, food, a subject on which she, customarily phlegmatic, was touchy.

In a family in which women run to fat, Juno was haggard. Incredibly, she had shared the family likeness. Her brash Jesuit brother, Theo – Theophane (the revelation of God) Archibald, destiny encoded in his name – returned from seminary at Louvain, Belgium to see her playing tennis in shorts. "Juno!" he cried. "You look like a fat Chettiah women!" She stopped eating until this was not the case. With raised eyebrows, the aunts told the story in unison, in a rhythmic, emphatic chorus. "No rice. No sugar. No fruit juice. No mangoes. Just water with a dash of lemon. And dry bread. Soon she was skin and bones. *Tell her*, Anita, tell her to eat. We're *so* worried about her."

* * *

We dutifully paid our visits – Ethel, Winifred, Priscilla, Eudora, Fulvia… Mangalorian names changed with each generation. Once Portuguese: My great-grandparents were Ligouri and Appolina Coelho, Jao Lobo, Salvador Mathias. Babies were, unimaginatively, given the name of the Parish Priest or the saint of the day, no matter how outlandish or otherworldly: Thrasius, Pulcheria, Paschalia, Balthazar, Blasius, Callistus, Faustin, Custudio, Seraphine, Boniface, Bonaventure, Cajetan, Clothilda. With the British Empire entrenched, Portuguese names faded, giving place to starched Victorian ones; fanciful raids on Shakespeare, Chaucer, Greek mythology and poetry, yielded Claudius, Gertrude, Ophelia, Leander, Griselda, Nympha, Christabel, Sybil and Nereus, the old man of the sea. A set of war siblings were impartially named Adolph (Dolphie), Winston and Joseph. Some played a single string, Oswald, Oscar, Orville, Odile Domingo; or Denise, Danny, Diane, Douggie, Denzil, and David, children of Dougie and Daphne Diaz. Or rhymed: the triplets, Asha, Isha, Usha; or the Pintos, Gilbert, Albert, Humbert, Cuthbert, Egbert and Norbert. Another set of Mathiases named their children alphabetically, like hurricanes, reluctantly stopping at Quentin, their seventeenth.

Those were the days of prodigious families, mothers and children pregnant together, nephews older than uncles. My father's neighbors, the P.G. D'Souzas ("the Blind Pig") had seventeen children, interchangeable with the fourteen Mathiases. Spotting my uncle Joe at her dining table, Mrs. D'Souza said vaguely, "Joe! you must come and stay with us some time." "I've been here for the last three days," he said. Neither mother had noticed!

In independent India, Anglicized names, Melroy, Gerson, Flavia were passé. "Graveyard names!" my father groaned. Under Hindu hegemony, many families, discovering ancestral memories of being Brahmin before their conversion half a millennium ago, replaced their "prestigious" names, Coelho, Lobo, Saldahna, Gonsalves, Mascarenhas, Rebello with old Brahminical surnames, so that a Mangalorean Kamath or Prabhu, say, probably indicates a Catholic. (Oddly, an extraordinary number of Catholic families claim descent from Tippu Sultan, the last ruler of the princely state of Mysore, putative progeny of "hanky-panky" in barns while he fled from the British.) Hindu first names or nicknames were in. My sister and cousins are Shalini, Nirmala, Ashok, Malati, Premila, though each has a nickname, originating in parental endearments, so the inner circle knew that Popsy was Premila; Chicky was Malati; Chippy, "a chip off the old block," was Michael, like his father, and Veronica was Buddie (old woman) – her father Sonny's teasing nick-name when she was a gawky gap-toothed six year old, ossified longer than baby teeth. Now, in the emigration generation, children mostly have "international names," Indian, but transcultural: Tara, Rohan, Sheila, Maya, Natasha, Anita, and, thanks to the Waste Land, Shanti.

So we visited all the family and friends, loved or hated, with whom we were on speaking terms, arriving unannounced, like the Magi – as was considered good manners: calling ahead would put the onus of preparation on the unoffending host, whereas if you just showed up, you took their manger or mansion as you found it. Like the Magi, we brought gifts – not frankincense, gold and myrrh, but halwa, pedas, and burfis. Someone was sure to be in. The people we visited lived on milk and honey, golden syrup and treacle, from stocks, factories, or the ancestral terraced plantations of cashew-nuts, pepper and coffee in the green hills around Mangalore on which the fortunes of several "old families" were built. All morning, all evening, we ate *neurios*, coconut-stuffed pasties; *chacklees*, spicy gram flour deep-fried in bristly snail spirals; *parthecums*, pungent banana chips; *kulkuls*, fried sugary dough rolled into shells on the back of a comb, and Christmas fruit cake with marzipan icing as we sat opposite plastic trees, sparkling with neon orbs, wreathed with popcorn or cotton wool snow, celebrating the weather of England rather than Bethlehem.

And talked of many things. Of blue chips, prices, politics, people, a great continuing Ring. Rhinegold: "Your uncle Morris is Director of United Breweries in Singapore now. Did you see the newspaper article about how that secretive Lee Kuan Yew sends him on private missions to Bombay?" Valkyries: "Your friend Faye, I remember when her mother eloped with that Protestant, a Soames, with only the clothes she had on. I even had to give her my blouses and petticoats." And in a conventionally lowered voice. "Your cousin Bernice's youngest boy; he doesn't resemble Hubert, have you noticed?" "Yeees." "Her lover's from a former princely family, she says. And poor Hubert's off in the god-forsaken northeast."

But, mostly, Gotterdamerung, crepuscular death, decay, doom. "I saw Debby, even weirder." "Debby?" "Debby C. – who married her first cousin, and had a breakdown on her honeymoon in Europe, after which she lived secluded on the family coffee estate, to which he occasionally returned to get her, once more, pregnant, while she grew stranger, dreamier." "Belita miscarried. So sad, her mother-in-law forced her to scrub the bathroom floors while she was pregnant." "S. has never recovered from his wife's death. On their honeymoon! Stepped into the elevator, expecting to find it there; fell into the shaft, broke her neck." "The Fathers have taken that drunken Willie in hand. Imagine, he beat up his sister, after she gave Anita those old classics." "Francis Xavier just had a heart attack." "Oh no! I'll never forget how he passed out at his daughter's grand engagement party – you know to that jerk from the States who dumped her. '*Sugar!*' he called – he's diabetic – and poured it into his mouth, straight from the bowl." "You know that druggie, Angelo. Goes to an ashram, declares himself a vegetarian, sits on his bed in some sort of trance; when he visited his aunt, Margaret, she, poor thing, took a plate of kichdi to him with just the tiniest bit of meat. He flung it on the floor, then continued staring at her with fixed, glassy eyes."

All this, good news, bad news, just news in English. Konkani – a hybrid of Portuguese and Marathi only spoken in Mangalore and Goa – is the nominal mother-tongue I neither speak nor understand; neither does my father. Since the nineteenth century, Catholic schools and universities have taught only in English; their products – everyone we visited – spoke it as, or almost as, a first language.

"I'll never retire in Mangalore," my father declared. "A sneeze at one end of the town is analyzed at the other." We visited my mother's aunt, Rosie Coelho (who seemed too good to be true, though she was true), smiling broadly with genuine sweetness, a woman in whom it was impossible to imagine guile or malice; benevolent, generous, gift-exchanging, to our embarrassment, the little box of sweets we gave her with a big basket of mangoes from her garden. And Mangalore is bright, benign Hobbiton.

But many a time, in the age of innocence, I naively walked into the sticky, tricky parlor of a Black Widow, who into her eighties and beyond, smiles and smiles and giggles girlishly, exuding sympathy and charm, offering appetizers with the "you know…" assumption of shared wisdom and virtue, sucking all of interest about you, about everyone you know, to then villainously disseminate relationship-wrecking rumors; who combats the loss of status, interestingness and power which age and widowhood bring by weaving a web of whispers and malignant lies, whom people placate lest they become her next meal – futile – for it is the nature of black widows to bite, except, sometimes, some of their children. Bitter? Bitten. For when I hear my blithe words bloodied, mangled, regurgitated almost unrecognizably from another black widow in her treacly web, I feel that I am in the land of Mordor where the shadows lie, and that small town was no Shire, but the old sow that eats its farrow, whose claustrophobia I must escape to live, to err, to fall, to triumph, to recreate life out of life!

Rosie's daughter, Martha, her grin wide, ingenuous, emerged in a housecoat, the Mangalorean woman's unbecoming at-home garb. She, toothless and wrinkled, didn't look much younger than her mother; like a baby or a saint, she was, without artifice, entirely herself. Ecstatic, electrifying gossip about Martha abounded; in fact, she told it herself.

"Ah *Baa* (Konkani for dearie). I can tell how shocked you are at how I look. I will not lie to you, Baa. It's because of my diet. I have beer for breakfast everyday, and Mummy sends for a little" (signing a square bracket) "whiskey for lunch and rum for dinner. But no more than that."

"But if I don't have that, I feel sick." Martha's sweet-faced Mummy stood by, like a statue of acceptant love, smiling a somewhat absent smile, as if she hadn't really heard what was being said, wasn't entirely there. My father and I listened, amazed; Martha was (improbably) the first cousin of my mother, whose most frequent expression, like that of her family's, was WWPT, "What will people think?"

Virginia Woolf, imagining the ignominy and madness that would have befallen Shakespeare's sister had she written, postulated, "Whenever we see a witch or a mad woman or a suicide, we see a thwarted poet." Martha muttered in her sleep in rhythm and rhyme. She got into a lawsuit with the Bishop who'd asked her to leave the house she rented from him; sheltering behind tenant-protection laws, she refused. She wrote doggerel to his minion: "Father Digby is a knave and goon; Father Digby has sealed his doom." "I wanted to write an anonymous letter, baa, but then – *I signed it*." Hired ruffians appeared, the usual way recalcitrant renters are evicted. "Baa, the walls were splattered with my blood. I lost all my front teeth."

The witch that came (the withered hag)/ Was once the beauty Abhishag... Her cousins told us Martha's story with controlled rage. She was, ominously, the best-natured of the cousins, honest, childlike, full of joie de vivre. Smart, cheeky and charming as a young woman, Martha had been the favorite of her father, my grandfather's brother, Dr. Coelho, Professor of Dermatology, revered, decorated, and famous for treating lepers for free. (He had left instructions for the most spartan of funerals to avoid that guilty one-upmanship with baked meats that can plunge a grieving family into penury and debt – thus giving people "permission" to go and do likewise: "If Dr. Coelho's family could..."). When she was young, married, well-connected, and Cabinet Ministers, even the Chief Minister of Karnataka, came to her parties, nuns and priests crowded her. "Come with us to the Chief Minister, Martha," they said. "Come to the Housing Minister. We have a request." She went. As an honored guest, she was served alcohol – which (in common with many Mangaloreans) happened to be her Achille's-heel, linden-leaf weakness. She drank – to be dropped as her beauty vanished and her marriage, her money and connections, everything but her mother. *No memory of having starred/ Can atone for later disregard/ Or keep the end from being hard.*

"I'd glad you behaved," my father grinned. "Aunt Rosie's sister, Dotty, was there." How young men and women giggled about the community's match-maker, plump, comfortable, uncomfortably named Dotty, and her little red Domesday Book with vital stats about every Mangalorean girl or boy who was anyone (giggled until they needed her services). Then parental whispers in corners, and gnomic Delphic utterances: "Tell her to lose weight." "Tell him to get a green card."

Dottie did not *charge* – "It gives me something to do; I like to help" – but, at weddings, she was a guest of honor, the bride's family gave her costly silk Kanjeeveram sarees, and...oh, nothing was too much before the couple who stood before the altar, beaming at each other with tenderness and wild hope, fully prepared to live happily ever after (which, surprisingly often, they did) rode off into the sunset with pleased punchy Cheshire cat smiles, as if it had all been their idea.

The dragon-guarded strait path to bliss: destiny hinged on luck, as well as on character. Two small town sisters or cousins: one might marry a successful physician or entrepreneur, in the U.S., say, and file among the world's spiffiest tax returns; her kids are successful; the other's spouse stays put, never realizes his ambitions, loses his small job, his health, drinks, drifts. And whose fault was that? "Behind, beneath, every successful man…"

Algebraic negotiations sought equilibrium between the ideal child-in-law and a realistically achievable one. Generations of family laundry, clean, dirty, lingered in communal memory; stalagmites of reputation grew from birth. Serpentine whispers doom: "His mother drinks." "A little…" a discreet tapping of the temples. Drunkenness, retardation, instability, insanity, were genetic, everyone knew; let the chattering classes chatter about heredity and environment; nature and nurture; Edwards and Jukes. Desiderata: in a boy, good family, money, a upwardly mobile career, "a sweet boy." In a girl: family, money, then (in that order) fairness and beauty; sundry accomplishments; "very sweet." Those with the greatest sum total of these married their counterparts. Which is probably what would have happened, though less scientifically, had the young people had been left to their own devices.

Dowry, receiving it, giving it, was banned by the Indian Supreme Court in 1961; sure! "The boy's family had all the expense of educating the boy; he'll look after the girl. Why shouldn't the girl's family contribute?" "But the girl's educated too!"

A snort, a shrug. That's the way things are.

No fixed figure. While Ms. Plain-Jane's parents might, as she neared the last-chance late twenties, in desperation offer a farm, in the seventies, it was an assortment of the "4 F's", phone, fridge, Fiat, flat (now videophones, medical clinics, resorts) beside jewelry and money, an invisible price tag somehow revealed, sometimes blatantly: my father told of a jeep ride through estates with a bride-seeking brother: "This will be yours, and this."

However, "the marriage market" was a human transaction, not sheerly a matter of the stock market, stock-breeding, and so the best stocked apple-carts of mother-in-laws and matchmakers gang oft agley. An infatuation with a long-lashed Adonis, or with a girl's beauty or bubbliness, might prevail despite the best advice. A double standard: as is universally true, plainness, or downright ugliness was more of a handicap for a woman. Our friends sent their daughter Odette to the Radcliffe Infirmary in Oxford to have her harelip corrected before she entered the marriage market. Her father, escorting her, had the surgery at the same time, though his had never mattered: *he* was an engineer. Here, as elsewhere, a woman whose face was her fortune married "up," despite class or accomplishments, and a rich woman did better than if her face had been her fortune. A few, as I did myself, side-stepped the whole thing, and had "love marriages." And "He was *caught*," everyone says bitterly.

Unlike Hindus who seek their true love through the Via Galactea, horoscopes, classified ads, grapevines, through an entire state, an entire nation, Mangalorean Catholics have pretty much married Mangalorean Catholics, local or diasporic, since they were converted in the early sixteenth century, and, what's more, married (often their own cousins) within their own snobbily defined class within which individuals, my husband and I, say, can trace multiple relationships. This carefully engineered eugenic mating over centuries, artificial selection in Darwin's terms, has, as intended, disproportionately strengthened desired traits: the coveted lighter skin and good features; intelligence; the ingenuity, doggedness, flair, or whatever, that produces wealth.

And the accidental, inevitable consequence: a community in which "the mad woman in the attic" was not just a literary stock character. "Look up discreetly," my father murmured as we passed the mansion of an old, wealthy, respected family. "Who was that Pa? She wasn't wearing....?

"Ssh. M's daughter, Margaret. She never mentions her daughter. Neither does anyone else. Though everyone knows. She keeps her locked up, though sometimes she gets to the window and…you saw."

Outwardly, the moonlight slept sweet upon the bank, and in the soft stillness and night, there was sweet harmony. Outwardly. But often, even in the snootiest families: a missing child, insane like Margaret (whose mother, cutting flowers, alerted by the gaping of passersby, ran upstairs to apprehend her); mildly retarded, or multiply disabled, euphemistically called "spastic," the fruit of genes bruised by five hundred years of a small, much-pooled gene pool, attributed to birth traumas. The siblings must get married.

Almost every old genteel Mangalorean family had their Peter Pan, called Baba or Baby into middle age, for whom the twentieth century proved too much: a coddled son or daughter, once of great promise, the community's pride, who, unable or unwilling to grab the trophy spouse, the trophies, still, in a chronic dazed breakdown, lived with Mummy in the bomb shelter of the family home they would eventually inherit. There were, here as elsewhere, sad spinsters and wistful bachelors who somehow missed "two for joy," and square pegs who slipped through cracked round holes, whose Medusa reflection parents and "well-wishers" brandished in a burnished shield before the rare eccentric. *Beware. Beware.*

I too have seen some of the best minds of my generation destroyed. Angelo, my cousin, famous among the nuns and priests of India, guinea-pigged by many Orders, subjected to every quack and craze, Charismatic healer, yogi, positive thinker, transaction analyst; to Gestalt, psychiatry, psychotherapy, inner healing. A chess champion, a proclaimed genius, as the promising young often are; achieving the highest aggregate in the State school-leaving exams, but with one misstep, a failure in compulsory Hindi, which meant a re-take, which never happened; instead, drugs, theosophy, a fling at being a rishi in an ashram, the occult; deep open-eyed trances; some swore he levitated. He looked like Death-in-Life, like one possessed, as he stared out of terrible, blighted eyes, hearing hissing Erinyes as his mind's circuits blew, and the plagues piled up – frustration, violence, institutionalization, suicide.

And, in Jamshedpur, the gentle, androgynous Mangalorian, Osbert, on whom every girl had a crush, long-fringed, long-haired, long-lashed like Paul McCartney, like the Beatles, whose songs he sang, twangy-voiced, strumming on his guitar, who went to

England on a Commonwealth scholarship (where, adding to his small town fame, he met the Duke of Edinburgh), who dabbled in drugs (for the impressionable, the Beatles, drugs, rock and roll were all one, while the cannier adopted the music, the hair-cuts, the batik, the cool until they took their place among the elders at the city gates). Drugs, adulterated?, excessive, which *whispered words of wisdom, let it be, let it be,* destroyed his mind, his fiber; now study, work, a steady job became pipe dreams.

So like others kept afloat by their parents' guilty broken hearts, he vanished behind his newspaper, lived with them until they died, their ironic silver lining, his immense good nature still evident on his blighted lost-boy face, whose fine features had grown flabby, for, eventually, character tells its tale. Once orphaned, he floated around town, a middle-aged wraith, chain-smoking, chain-drinking tea in grimy dhabas, finally growing so disheveled, shaggy, unwashed, sun-scorched, that, when he tried to visit my parents, the guard would not let him past the gate. Another sixties refrain: Joan Baez, *And there but for fortune, go you or I, mmm, mmm.*

* * *

My sister and I, reunited after a month, compared notes. We were then the only Coelho grandchildren, but just another two among the twenty-seven Mathias cousins. While my Christmas Eve prayers for good presents fell on rocky soil, producing twenty-five rupees from my grandmother to split with my sister and that Five Star bar, the trade winds of family love wafted Shalini toys and cash, clothes and candy. To forestall inevitable tears, my father, each Christmas in Mangalore, flashed a Learian promise, "Ask for whatever you want, and I'll give it to you." "Four slabs of Cadbury's chocolate, four Agatha Christies, and a Monopoly set!" I stipulated, and got them – and then, as if to counteract the spoils and spoiling of Bombay, he forgot to get my sister a present. "But look what *Pa* gave me!" I said, gazing sadly at her presents. "What did Pa give you?" She cried; my mother glared at him, and dispatched him to get her a present, but since we already had Monopoly, he got her a cheaper Indian version, Trade, with Bombay properties, Nepean

Sea Drive, Malabar Hill and Juhu Beach, rather than Fleet Street, Chelsea, and the Strand. "I got Monopoly; you got Trade."

3 | Zigzags

Flames leaped into the horizon. My parents, my sister, Shalini, and I abandoned our dinner to race up to the terrace and watch the blaze. It was Holi, the Hindu spring festival, an explosion of mischief celebrating the god Krishna's shenanigans with the cowgirls. Flung water balloons gushed vermilion; water pistols squirted indigo. Stranger smeared stranger with silver paint stolen from construction sites. Buckets – dishwater? urine? – were emptied from high apartment windows onto passersby. Riotousness and devilry burst forth, a ripe sore.

Durga, our tiny, curly-haired cook, cycled into town and returned, panting with news. A procession of Hindus, chanting bhajans, statues of Shiva, god of destruction, hoisted on their shoulders, had marched past the mosque and forced a pig into it. Rumors of Muslim vengeance for this desecration flew round the town. "I won't tell you in front of the chhota memsahibs," Durga said. The Hindus retaliated. Jamshedpur, my North Indian home town, was 82 percent Hindu and 11 percent Muslim. The fire engines were silent as Muslim slums, homes, and businesses burned.

Mesmerized by the flames zigzagging into the horizon, I sat on the parapet, my legs dangling over the edge. In the boredom of boarding school, I had read of front-page disasters wistfully – hurricanes, earthquakes, landslides, floods, war. But nothing happened, except in the movies. I was seventeen and had just graduated from Saint Mary's Convent, Nainital, a century-old boarding school in the Himalayas run by German and Irish nuns – staid, staid.

I gazed down: fire devouring houses, crashing rafters, distant screaming. The effect was hypnotic, as in a cinema rustling with peanut-crunching, betel-nut chewing, enthralled throngs. But these were not sound effects – I snapped out of reverie – these were real people, just like me, burning to death. Suddenly sickened, I ran downstairs and locked myself in my room.

The police slapped a curfew on the town: A glare, a curse, a flung stone could spark a riot. Police stood at every street corner, their rifles cocked. The market shut down. Home deliveries of bread and milk stopped. The cook sifted out insects to make parathas from old whole wheat flour. It was romantic in a way, the Indian Family Robinson.

The Hindu-Muslim riots held little personal terror: I was Roman Catholic. My forebears from Mangalore on the west coast of India were converted in the mid-sixteenth century by Portuguese missionaries, backed by the Inquisition. It was the prospect of boredom that bothered me. At the first hint of violence, libraries closed their stacks as too-easy targets for arsonists. Though we lived in faculty housing on the campus of Xavier Labor Relations Institute, a business school run by American Jesuits at which my father taught, it was impossible to get books. How would I get through curfew without them? A compulsive reader, I went through our bookshelves: Jane Eyre, Wuthering Heights, I had read them several times. I shrank from rereading The Return of the Native, Far from the Madding Crowd, or The Mill on the Floss, though I loved those "classics."

I settled down with the books I had not already read: Christian books. My father bought them at parish jumble sales as though there were virtue in the purchase. He never read them. To my surprise, I was fascinated. The Cross and the Switchblade, David Wilkerson's tale of Christ's radiance transforming young gangsters and drug addicts in New York City, and Catherine Marshall's Beyond Ourselves were vivid accounts of Christ bursting into everyday life, setting it to music, making it sweet. This felt very different from the fossilized Catholicism forced on us at boarding school.

My childhood had been totally immersed in Catholicism – saints, angels, rosaries, novenas, litanies. It was punctuated with those rituals – baptism, first confession, first Communion, confirmation – that can so entwine themselves with the fabric of your spirit that to slough off Catholicism is to shiver in uncertainty. It's like stripping off your skin. As a child, I unquestioningly accepted Catholicism, and believed what I was taught; that it was the only true faith. Extra ecclesiam nulla salus: Outside the church, there is no salvation.

When I was eleven, I read through a compendium of General Knowledge during the winter school holiday and discovered a new passion: Greek mythology. I abandoned my stamp and postcard collections to read everything I could find on the enchanted universe of Greek gods and goddesses. Then, I chanced upon an idea that shattered my religious complacency.

I read that primitive men and women, often devastated by nature, imagined it was God. They worshiped the sun as Apollo; corn, fickle in blight or plenty, was Ceres; the raging sea, they imagined, was the mighty god Poseidon; the north wind, Boreas. Flabbergasted mortals elevated the forces of erratic, uncontrollable nature into gods to adore and placate. I understood. And was Catholicism any different from this awe-struck, foolish approach to nature? I doubted it.

I became an atheist and fed off the secret knowledge of intellectual superiority. How benighted they were, these parents, grandparents, priests, and nuns who ran our boarding school-they and their rattling rosary beads and boring Masses, their sprinklings of holy water from Lourdes, their relics, holy pictures, apparitions of the Virgin, prayers both to and for any good soul that left this earth. Just eleven, I knew better. I whispered to cronies, "I am an atheist," as one might confide, "I am a murderess."

Sister Hermine, our stern-faced, square-jawed German principal, summoned her rebellious charges to her office and, from her lowest desk drawer, slowly drew forth her strap-a thick strip of leather. She rarely had to use it. At the mere sight, the victim whimpered in terror and repentance. I was the only girl she had ever strapped, Sister Hermine often said, shaking her head. When I was sent to the principal's office to apologize for calling Miss Fernandes – a teacher who had maliciously and unfairly punished me – a Gorgon and a bitch, I clarified "No, I didn't call her a bitch. I said a witch," which seemed worse. Since I refused to recant (I meant what I'd said) I was struck on the calves with the strap and let off apologizing. Sister Hermine was ambivalent about breaking her students' wills. "What's the merit in taming lambs?" my father's brother, Theo Mathias, a Jesuit, asked her when she was close to expelling me. "But if you get a lion cub, and tame it into a lamb, isn't that something to be proud of?" Sister Hermine agreed.

Still, she would be unimpressed by an eleven-year-old atheist, I thought. Outwardly, I went through enforced Catholicism-daily Mass; Benediction: a cascade of hymns every Sunday evening; adoration: silent prayer before the Blessed Sacrament every first Sunday; confession, rosary, stations of the cross, and choir practices. Inwardly, I scoffed, and as the habit of confidence grew, I rebelled. I got my friends to join me in crawling out of the choir room while Sister Cecilia, behind the organ, warbled in a holy dream. I embedded the altar candles at Mass with the sulfurous heads of match sticks, reducing the girls who strained to catch the hiss, the sputter, the odor, to convulsive giggles.

When I turned fourteen – no longer one of the "babies," or the "middle set," but a "big girl," especially in my own estimation – I knocked on Sister Hermine's door and announced that I did not believe in Catholicism, or in God for that matter, so please, please, could I not have to be a Catholic, and – especially – not have to go to church?

"I'd much rather join the non-Catholics at 'silent occupation,'" I protested. The Hindus, Muslims, and Sikhs were allowed to read, study, paint, or embroider, provided they sat at their desks in perfect silence – oh, oasis! – while we, we went to church.

"Can't I just obey the Ten Commandments and not go to church?" I asked.

She was amused. "What are the Ten Commandments?"

I rattled them off from years of catechism, but stumbled over "Thou shalt not covet thy neighbor's wife." "See, you can't even say the Ten Commandments. How can you obey the Ten Commandments?" Sister Hermine laughed. "You have to be a Catholic now. Wait until you are twenty-one. Then decide."

And that was that. I got no support from my parents for my desire to officially "lapse." They detested adverse attention. You are a Catholic, my mother said, whether you like it or not. Seven years to go.

I became openly defiant. As president of the debating club, I chose subjects like "God is dead," and "religion is the opiate of the people," speaking for the motion, annoying the nuns. My favorite writers were Matthew Arnold and Thomas Hardy. (I was not aware that doubt had a more modern face.) I embraced Hardy's bleak Learian vision – "As flies to wanton boys are we to the gods; they kill us for their sport" – his absent or malign god.

Still, the vanishing of God left a vacuum which was filled by restlessness, unhappiness, and puzzlement about the purpose of life. Like Ivan in The Brothers Karamazov, I concluded that if there was no God, there was also no immutable moral law, nothing intrinsically right or wrong. There was no one to reward goodness or punish wrongdoing in this world, and there was no world to come. So one could do whatever one wanted or, at least, whatever one could get away with.

I shared my new philosophy with my friends. We formed a gang, "the bandits," and our first exploit was our daily raids on Modern Store which catered to rich kids from the four expensive boarding schools in Nainital, and to the tourists and honeymooners who swamped the Himalayan resort. Kaye, Savneet, Bella, and I strolled into the store wearing the baggy sweaters of our convent uniform, designed to disguise nubile figures. We stuffed Cadbury's chocolate, Mills and Boon romances, stickers, cards, nail polish, and costume jewelry into our sleeves and up our sweaters. When our desks overflowed, the nuns noticed, made inquiries, then pounced on us. We were marched back to the shop with our booty and forced to apologize: "We are sorry, 'Mr. Modern.'"

Furious, I debated with my class teacher, the fiery, Irish Sister Josephine, through a long summer evening. Perched on a piano in the music room (a sacrilege), I argued that if "Mr. Modern" overcharged us all year, it was okay to even things occasionally by "swacking" from him. Her beautiful brown eyes kindled. "The Bible says..." she began. But I did not believe the Bible was "the Word of God," indisputable.

But at the same time – secretly – I began to crave a moral framework. How easy choice can be when there are absolutes, a road map through the maze of decisions. How wearying to thrash out the morality of every case, every time, all by yourself. I wished I could believe.

"You are experiencing an Augustinian restlessness," Sister Josephine said, quoting the saint: "Thou hast made us for Thyself, O Lord, and our hearts are restless until they rest in you." Pascal, she said, wrote of the "God-shaped vacuum" only God could fill. And I was God-bitten. Atheism is closer to faith than indifference is.

I was nicknamed "the naughtiest girl in school" after an Enid Blyton heroine. But being a rebel wasn't really fun despite its jaunty aura. If I could have been "good," I would have. When the nuns predicted a conversion experience for me, I feared it. I wanted it. Their naughtiest girls often become the "holiest," they claimed. For was not Saint Augustine a rake, and Saint Francis a playboy, and, as for Saint Mary Magdalen...?

When we were to be confirmed, I was eleven. Sister Magdalene, an enormous, squint-eyed British nun, persuaded me to take her name. "Mary Magdalen was a notorious sinner who became very holy. Take her name, and she will ask God to give you the grace of a great conversion," she said. The old story-flamboyant rebellion later swinging to passionate devotion. I did not ask "Maggie" why she compared me to a supposed prostitute, harbor to seven demons. I composed scandalous poems about the nuns: "Sister Secunda eloped with a gunda," a bandit. I ran away from school with Micky, the school sheepdog. In revenge for being sent out of class, I locked my teacher and classmates into the classroom throughout an afternoon. Such things were surely wicked. But too awkward, alas, too "nice," to refuse Sister Magdalene, I became Anita Mary Magdalene Mathias, adopting that stodgy, dated name I hated. The classic coming-to-faith trajectory had its appeal. I wondered if the "Mary Magdalen" might prove prophetic. Would I suddenly turn "good," perhaps even, in a blaze of glory, become "a great saint"?

I might convert like Paul. A bullet of hatred, galloping to Damascus to kill and destroy, he is struck off his horse and glimpses divinity. "Saul, Saul, it is hard for you to kick against the goad." "Who are you, Lord?" "I am Jesus whom you persecute." His life acquires a purpose: "the surpassing greatness of knowing Jesus

Christ, my Lord." "For me to live is Christ, to die is gain," he writes. How wonderful, I thought, to convert just like that, your life transformed-but I lacked both belief and an object of devotion.

Father Clement Campos and Father Ivo Fernandes, handsome Redemptorist priests with twangy-voiced charm, preached our annual retreats: an aesthetic delight, days of hymns and silences, resounding oratory, and prayer by candlelight led by a luscious male voice. And every year we, who from March to December rarely saw a man except the chaplain, developed monstrous, predictable crushes.

"And is anyone here an atheist?" the priest asked provocatively on the first retreat evening as he polled our group of Catholics, Hindus, Muslims, Sikhs, Jains, Buddhists – and atheists. And every year, I raised my hand.

For the next week, they worked on me – private conferences and counseling, private prayers for healing from whatever trauma brought me, a Catholic girl of good family, to this strange pass. A foot away from the man's animated brown eyes, how easy conversion seemed; how it would please this appealing priest.

"Get up at 5 a.m. tomorrow," the priest said, "and sit alone. Watch the sun rise on those snow-tipped mountains and ask yourself, 'Could this grandeur come to be by accident?'" So I raised my eyes to the Himalayas, waiting to be surprised by faith. Gazing up at the mountains, I thought, as I was expected to-"Maybe, maybe...." But back down in the valley, any belief born of eloquence and hormones left with the good-looking priest.

Still, I was fertile soil at seventeen as I read the Bible while confined to the house during those Hindu-Muslim riots. On the patio where I sat reading, the sun, a ball of vermilion fire, sank beneath the emerald fortress of trees, lit by the orange-crimson flowers of the Flame of the Forest and the red and yellow Royal Poinciana. I continued reading after dusk by the glow of a kerosene lamp. Was Jesus Christ who the New Testament claimed he was: the God who made and loves us, the creator of the universe, cornerstone and crux of human history, the zigzag of the jigsaw that makes sense of everything else?

Paul says, "He is the image of the invisible God. All things were created by him and for him... and in him all things hold together."

And Jesus asked them, "Who do you say that I am?" And Peter answered, "You are the Christ, the son of the Living God."

Who do you say that I am? Who do you say that I am? Driven by an inchoate hunger, I read and reread the New Testament, my thirst growing even as it was quenched. Gradually, my cherished objections-the lack of scientific proof; the myth-like aspects of virgin birth and a Christ resurrected from the dead; that Christianity was the credulity of fishermen given form and credibility by Paul's sophisticated intellect – crumbled like clay gods. No, this was not mythology. It differed from the tales of Mount Kailash, Mount Olympus, and Asgard that I had devoured. It differed in the sense of, well, holiness. It had the taste of truth. Jesus' words sang in me like music, like poetry. I found myself praying, "Lord, I believe. Help thou my unbelief."

I gradually surrendered the intellectual high ground of cold reason: What I do not see with my eyes, or feel with my hands, I will not believe. I could not spar against the Christ I apprehended dimly – I who did not understand cars, or logarithms, or tides, or love. It's possible the Gospels are true, I conceded. It's plausible. Intellect can bring you to the brink of belief. Faith is the missing link. I believed: in a leap of the heart as rationally inexplicable as the leap from affection to love. For like love, faith is the heart's knowledge. "Lord," I prayed. "I believe. You are the living God. I will follow you, wherever you lead. I will do your will insofar as you make it clear to me what it is." I did not quail at this largesse, this scattering of blank checks. I did not add, "but be merciful, Lord. Be sensible." With an air of adventure, of rusty doors wrenched from their sockets, revealing fresh vistas, I prayed: "Show me, Lord. What should I do?"

I would dedicate my life to Christ, I decided. How then should I live? "A life of love!" How exactly, I did not know, but, being seventeen, I wanted to do something dramatic and do it swiftly. "I want to be a pen in God's hands," I wrote in my journal, "picked up and used, leaving light where I have written."

My first impulse, to fly off from Jamshedpur to help David Wilkerson of The Cross and the Switchblade in his work with teen drug addicts and gangsters in Harlem, wasn't exactly practical. While casting about for a vocation, I volunteered in the Cheshire Home for physically handicapped and mentally retarded children, on the outskirts of Jamshedpur. Here, in the postage stamp of my world, I tried to practice the kindness at the heart of Christianity, without which words are noisy gongs, ardor and alms worth little. I lived with the Vincent de Paul nuns and was captivated by their life of prayer, quiet work, and silences. "How beautiful this serene life is, governed by the pealing of bells," I wrote in my journal. "Scaling inward mountains – lovelier by far than a life of distraction, worries, gossip, and moneymaking, a life inimical to the spirit."

Catholic children brought up by nuns or priests brace themselves against a vocation: a tap on the shoulder, inward marching orders, an imperative you can ignore, but at the cost of your soul. At some time, we all think we've caught it: That's it, we are the chosen of God, chosen for a lonely, lovely way, another bride of Christ.

Now, I began, obsessively, to wonder if I had a religious vocation. God was the only thing that was real, I kept reminding myself, and all else – college, marriage, career, social life, money-was vanity. I wanted to find a way to live, always, close to Christ, tasting his joy and peace. Surely leaving "the world," becoming a nun, was the only way to do that.

While at the Cheshire Home, I read Edward Le Joly's Servant of Love about Mother Teresa's congregation, the Missionaries of Charity. How utterly radical they were in their following of Christ, I thought, as I read of their austere life, stripped down to essentials. They owned but two saris, a Bible, and no more than could fit into a bucket – their "suitcase" when they traveled. How seductive to slough off everything, to live deep in the embrace of Christ, the creator of the universe, friend sufficient for every need. Wow! Without training, with impetuosity, they plunged into all manner of human misery, their reach widening year by year, their mandate simply to serve "the poorest of the poor," defined broadly: lepers in Yemen, shut-ins in Melbourne, crazed drug addicts in New York, freezing homeless people in London, orphans in Peru, tramps near the Vatican, the dying destitute in Calcutta. The energy of it all and, unconsciously, I guess, the prospect of adventure dazzled me. They did just what Christ commanded, I thought, impressed: I was hungry and you gave me something to eat, I was sick and you looked after me. Whatsoever you do to the least of my brethren, that you do unto me. I felt an inner push, a shove toward this congregation, so literal in its imitation of Christ.

In a burst of headstrong lucidity, I sloughed off the destiny my parents had mapped for me: college, followed by (an arranged) marriage. No, I would become a Missionary of Charity. I would help those unable to help themselves. I would feed constantly off the light and joy of Jesus. The notion glowed.

Minutes after I'd returned from the Cheshire Home, full of bright decision, I announced it to my parents. I left the room swiftly as I saw my father's face freeze. My mother followed me. "Go and see your father." The muscles of his face worked. There were tears on his cheeks. "Why must you bounce from one extreme to another?" he asked. "You've always found it impossible to conform. In the convent, 'It's yours not to reason why.' It will be a life of exhausting manual work. Mother Teresa recruits simple women from the villages and you're an intellectual snob. You'll have nothing in common with them. Your mind will atrophy. You will be bored!

"However, if you are sure that God is calling you to this..." he acquiesced eventually. "But go slow. Be sure. Wait." Wait! "I will not wait," I said. "I will call them today. I have heard my vocation."

I left for the convent that August, feeling, with the naiveté of late adolescence, holier already, as if the Christian's life task of "being conformed to the image of Christ" could be accomplished in a dramatic grab for holiness, and showy, though worthy, doing would speed the slow, almost imperceptible process of transformation called sanctification. I grew. I grew through the next two years, through the aspirancy, postulancy, and novitiate. I grew through work in the orphanage, with the mentally retarded and the dying destitute; through prayer and Scripture study; through friendships and conflicts and the "testing of vocations," and through the tears and humiliation. And I grew through sickness and exhaustion that never let up, and eventually made the whole enterprise untenable, and which, after I left, was diagnosed as tuberculosis.

I left the convent sadly, with a sense of falling off, to study English as an undergraduate at Oxford University, to go to graduate school in creative writing in America, and later to forge myself into a writer and a faculty wife in suburban America-the less poetic path. I still see Christ as the wisdom that created the universe. I still see following him as the sanest way to live, a way I am committed to. The Christian imperatives which Jesus with his Gordian-knot-slashing directness reduced to two-to love God mightily and to love your neighbor as yourself-remain the same. There is just more distraction. The traditional monastic disciplines-prayer, meditation, adoration, the beautiful liturgy of the hours, and "spiritual reading"-served to draw one's thoughts back to Christ, the breadth and depth of his love, and his enabling grace. It now takes ingenuity to carve for myself a circle of silence to feed on Scripture and the transforming presence of Christ it houses, and to live contemplatively, mindful of Jesus not only amid the beauty and tranquillity of my garden, my writing, and my books, but amid a child's cries and crankiness, the crucible of marriage, and the haste and busyness which haunts America as poverty haunts India. Nurturing two young children, creating a loving family life, running a peaceful household – the demands to give of oneself are constant, without the convent's periodic sanctioned escape into the sacred ivory spaces of psalmody and song. In fact, I now consider domesticity, marriage, and motherhood a smithy in which the soul can be forged as painfully, as beautifully, as amid the splendid virginal solitudes of the convent.

4 | The Holy Ground of Kalighat

To Mercy, Pity, Peace and Love,
All pray in their distress:
And to these virtues of delight
Return their thankfulness.

For Mercy has a human heart
Pity, a human face:
And Love, the human form divine,
And Peace, the human dress.

William Blake, *Songs of Innocence*

Kalighat, the Home for the Dying Destitute was the toughest assignment in the convent, reputedly reserved for the mature. I kept asking for it until I got it: I was greedy for challenge. The place glowed in the light of literature. It had been written about, repeatedly. I had read the poetic accounts of Malcolm Muggeridge, Desmond Doig, and Edward Le Joly; I *had* to work there.

In 1952, Mother Teresa conceived the notion that the *dharmasala*, the dormitory for pilgrims to Calcutta's famous Kali temple, would make an ideal Home for the Dying Destitute. The municipality of Calcutta refused to turn over a portion of a famous Hindu pilgrimage site (after which Calcutta is named) to an obscure group of Christian nuns. Undaunted, Mother Teresa and her sisters accompanied by Father Henry, their chaplain, and lay Catholics marched through Calcutta's streets from six to nine each evening. They chanted the rosary and novenas, praying to be permitted to take in dying homeless people from the streets and nurse them in the dormitory of the Kali temple. The publicity worked in their favor. (Mother had a supernatural explanation.) A wing of Kalighat, the temple of Kali, a devouring, destructive goddess, was handed over to Mother Teresa. She rechristened it *Nirmal Hriday* in Bengali, The Immaculate Heart, in honor of Mary, conceived without sin. In the temple, Kali-worship continues, goats sacrificed daily amid chanting and singing.

In Hindu iconography, Kali, the Black One, is a hideous, black-faced hag, smeared with blood, her teeth are bared, her mocking tongue protrudes. She is naked except for her ornaments – a garland of skulls and a girdle of severed heads. Her four hands brandish a sword, a shield, a dangling head, and a strangling noose; her symbol is the ill-omened left-hand swastika. Until the nineteenth century, the "Thugs," a religious organization that murdered and robbed in the service of Kali, made ritual sacrifices of their victims at this temple. A male child was sacrificed every Friday evening.

The head priest of Kalighat had opposed the occupation of his temple by these Christian nuns. Groups of angry Hindu youngsters threatened Mother Teresa's Missionaries of Charity. They burst in and broke furniture, to the terror of the patients. The head priest of the Kali Temple – supposed to be a celibate *Brahmachari* – had a son he did not acknowledge, the story goes. That son, dying of tuberculosis at twenty-four, sat begging outside the Kali Temple, coughing blood, a dread shadow, scrupulously avoided. Looking out from the temple window, the priest saw the sisters lift his son onto a makeshift stretcher and carry him into their section of the temple. "How can they touch him, or stand to be near him?" he said. "These Missionaries of Charity must be genuinely good people, not Christian fanatics." He stopped opposing them. The sisters retained their wing of Kalighat which is now Mother Teresa's best-known home, almost as famous as the Kali Temple.

We entered the quietness of Kalighat after a long Jeep trip through Calcutta's streets, raucous with the incessant horns, the animated vendors, the high-decibel blare of radios with film songs barreling from megaphones,. We recited the rosary above the din around the Jeep as the rule decreed we should, no matter how unpropitious our surroundings. Our voices growing hoarse and our throats parched, we trolled through the fifteen "mysteries" of the life of Christ: *Joyful, Sorrowful,* and *Glorious.*

This chanting was meant to serve as a barricade against distraction and doubt. Just as well perhaps. While we hurtled through the honking and furor of buses and cars, the cackle of the red rubber horns on the three-wheeled autos called "bone-shakers" and snaked amid stray dogs I sometimes saw hit (willfully? out of unfathomable malice?) it was not easy to clasp simple verities: There is a God, that God loves me, as he loves every human on this crazy street. It was easier to believe that God had hurled the world into motion and then absconded, a notion I had heard denounced from the pulpit as atheistical absurdity.

Hail Mary, full of grace; the Lord is with you. Blessed are you among women, and blessed is the fruit of your womb, Jesus, we chanted as our Jeep swerved through street children, trams, lorries, motor-cycles, scooters, and dangerously lurching buses with youths leeching onto windows, railings, and roof. I usually kept my eyes closed. Calcutta was unnerving to a small-town girl. To open them was to contemplate the possibility, no, the probability, that our driver would collide with rickshaws dragged by scrawny men who looked tubercular and crammed with housewives and their purchases; hit a sacred cow, crush a child, and so cause an ugly communal riot for us to sort out. I remembered the time my father had to bail out a Jesuit professor, his colleague, who was nearly lynched for hitting a poor Hindu boy with his posh car.

Entering Kalighat is akin to entering a city church – or, for that matter, The Missionaries of Charity's chapel at Mother House in the center of Calcutta. You are stunned into stillness, into a sudden awareness of your jerky breath, your distracted mind. The silence shrouds you until you are aware that it is not silence, not really: there is the rustle of supplicants, rosary beads rattle, bowed heads breathe. So, in Kalighat, after your jangled spirit laps up apparent silence, you hear soft sounds – low moaning, a tubercular cough, patients tossing in pain and restlessness.

Still, Kalighat felt like holy ground. I often sensed the presence of God in the dimness and hush of that place. *Bhogobaan ekane acche*, Mother Teresa whispered in Bengali as she goes from bed to bed: *God is here*. Her creased face looked sad and sweet. This is *Bhogobaan ki badi*, God's house, the sisters tell new arrivals, believing that Kalighat is sanctified in its very stones by the thousands who have died peaceful deaths there. Perhaps the light created this aura. The light spilled from high windows through a filigreed lattice, spilled into the dim room with a stippled radiance that made working there epiphanic, an annunciation.

In this place Malcolm Muggeridge, curmudgeonly Catholic convert, experienced what he calls "the first authentic photographic miracle" as he filmed a B.B.C. documentary on Mother Teresa in 1969. The cameraman insisted that filming was impossible inside Kalighat – dimly lit by small windows high in the walls – but reluctantly tried it. In the processed film, the part taken inside was bathed in "a soft, exceptionally lovely light," whereas the rest, taken in the outside courtyard as an insurance, was dim and confused. Muggeridge writes: "I am absolutely convinced that this technically unaccountable light is Newman's 'Kindly Light.' The love in Kalighat is luminous like the halos artists have seen and made visible around the heads of saints. It is not at all surprising that this exquisite luminosity should register on a photographic film."

Perhaps Kalighat had that sense of being holy ground because it was an ancient Hindu pilgrimage site. I wondered whether the devotion of generations of Hindus, no less than Catholics, had hallowed the ground. Surely, I reasoned, all kinds of God-hunger are acceptable to Christ who chose as his symbols bread and wine, who offered his flesh to eat, his blood to drink. Perhaps what happens in a pilgrimage spot is not that God descends to earth in a shower of radiance and the earth ever after exudes his fragrance. Perhaps it is we who make spots of earth sacred when we bring our weary spirits, our thwarted hopes, the whole human freight of grief, and pray – our eyes grown wide and trusting; our being, a concentrated yearning. Perhaps that yearning – which is a glimpse of better things – makes that spot sacred and lingers in the earth and air and water so that future pilgrims say, "God is here."

On our way to work, we frequently picked people off the pavements where they lay and transported them to Kalighat to die, in Mother Teresa's phrase, "within sight of a kind face." "Stop," we cried to the driver, who then helped us carry them into the Jeep. (Occasionally we picked up a drunk who cursed us on his return to consciousness.) Most people we picked up were as emaciated as famine victims; they lay limp on the pavements, a feeble hand outstretched for alms. And yet there was no famine in Calcutta; our Prime Minister protested that nobody, simply nobody, dies of starvation in India.

These people had probably worked all their lives. But in a land where not every one can find work, and the wages paid are often not enough to live on, survival is everything. Saving money for an illiterate worker is an impossible dream. The poor have no insurance; there is no social security. "Naked they came into the world, naked they depart," as Job mourned. Many end their lives destitute on Calcutta's streets. They waste away as they grow too old, weak, or sick to scavenge for themselves or even root for food in the open garbage dumps.

For these people who are kicked aside, cursed and ignored, Kalighat is an inexplicable miracle, a last-minute respite, a stepping into grace. In her speeches, Mother loves to quote the dying man she brought to Kalighat from the streets of Calcutta – "All my life I have lived like a dog, but now I die like an angel" – which was, perhaps, just what he said, or, perhaps, a composite of many experiences.

Kalighat consists of two L-shaped wards, accommodating about sixty men and women, rows of low cots, snuggled even into every cranny. The Missionary Brothers of Charity, the male branch of the order founded by Brother Andrew, an Australian ex-Jesuit, help in the male ward; they sponge patients, change soiled clothes, hack off elongated and hardened toe-nails. I saw them as I entered the male ward to dispense medication – sweet, serious, humble and hardworking men. Perhaps I perceived them in cliches since I never actually talked to them. A novice hobnobbing with men would not have been approved of. We novices mainly worked in the female ward, an oblong room bathed in dim light from the beautiful white filigreed windows.

Iris, a tubercular Anglo-Indian patient, was Kalighat's presiding Fury. She hobbled all over the ward on her walking stick which she thrashed around when enraged. Her puckered brown face was a maze of hate-lines, and as she limped, she cursed: "Those bloody Muddses, I hate those swine, they..." "What's the matter, Iris?" people asked, mocking her – for every one, of course, knew her story by heart and was fed up of it. And as if it were new every morning, she'd repeat her tale of the Muddses, her distant relatives, this family she had helped who, in her old age, assaulted her, evicted her from her house, and pushed her down the stairs so that she broke her leg.

"Those bloody Muddses," she muttered, her rosary of hate. She was fond of me and would stroke me, telling me that I was nice, her smile surprisingly sweet. Every one had to be very good to me when Iris was around, or she would brandish her stick at them, reprimanding, "No, this is a *nice* sister." Poor Iris, balladeer of old grievances, anger always at boiling point for old wrongs. Her grudges had driven her crazy, cruel Furies devastating her long past the initial injury. I often talked to her, asking about her childhood in pre-Independence India, to try to divert her mind from the injustices over which it obsessively brooded to happier memories. I realized how wise Mother Teresa was when she admonished, "Forgive. Never allow yourself to become bitter. Bitterness is like cancer; it feeds on itself. It grows and grows."

I tried to feed a round-faced old lady, who was too weak to feed herself. She could barely swallow her rice. She kept pushing away my hand that waited with the next spoonful. I relaxed; I could see that I would be sitting on the edge of her bed for a long time. So while I tried to feed her, we talked. Her son had deposited her on the streets from where the sisters had eventually picked her up. "I haven't seen my four sons for years," she cried, her meal still uneaten.

I gave up on the rice and fed her the mango. She loved that. She fixed her eyes on the diminishing fruit, then asked for more. There was no more. So I folded the skin in two and drew it between her lips, again and again, until she had sucked the last drops of juice. Suddenly, her eyes lit up with love. Tears ran down her face. She caught me, pulled me to her, and rocked me in an embrace, crying, "Ma. Ma. Ma," her mind reverting to childhood, her face grown baby-sweet.

I hugged her back, not even trying to remember if she was tubercular, forgetting my mask and *Mycobacterium tuberculosis* spread by the respiratory route. During that insomniac night, I thought of her. The next evening, I sneaked out a mango from the convent kitchen and concealed it in my saree. I went straight to her bed. It was covered with a white sheet. She had died in the night.

Death was a constant in Kalighat, that Home in the temple of the goddess of death. Only the ostensibly dying were admitted. About half recovered with rest, medication, and nourishing food. For the rest, this was the end. When we entered the ward, stark white sheets, the color of mourning in India, covered the beds of those who had died the previous night. In the face of death, its inevitability, how trivial much of life seemed. "Teach us to number our days," the Psalmist cried, "that we may apply our hearts unto wisdom." I realized why the novice-mistresses preached detachment to us. *Guard your heart*, I admonished myself, chary of emotional involvement with one who might soon be a corpse in the morgue or burnt to ashes on the shore of the River Ganges.

In a place like Kalighat, perspective is everything. My parents, on their monthly visits, grumbled that it was a grim place, daunting and unpleasant – and so it is until its strange charm, its eerie radiance, works on you. I loved Kalighat for its tiny miracles. An old, almost bald woman with a wicked, shriveled face occupied a bed in a corner. Everyone avoided her: she was nasty. When she could sit up, she'd curse all within earshot. She spat gobs of yellow phlegm all over the floor, perversely ignoring her spittoon. Once, as I tried to feed her, she lost her temper and slapped me, sending my glasses flying across the ward.

Dealing with her was not a pleasure. So the other patients had often eaten their dinners and fallen asleep while she hadn't been brought her tray of gruel and boiled vegetables. One evening, chiding myself for my fastidiousness, I braced myself and took her tray to her. As I approached, she smiled, and her face briefly became numinous. It glowed. No one had ever seen her smile. I hugged the memory to myself as a shaft of grace, a cryptic divine sign – though perhaps it was a trick of the light.

But I remembered Gerard Manley Hopkins, my favorite poet:

> ...*Christ plays in ten thousand places,*
> *Lovely in limbs, and lovely in eyes not his*
> *To the Father through the features of men's faces.*

Most patients in Kalighat, too old or weak to walk, crept around the ward or to the bathroom while squatting on their haunches, slowly moving one tired leg after the other. Since their diseases were highly infectious – cholera, typhoid, and, especially, tuberculosis – we had to be vigilant. Sister Luke, the stern-faced nurse from Mauritius who ran Kalighat, ordered us to use masks all the time that we were in the ward. These we sewed ourselves, a double strip of thick cotton cloth, covering the nose and mouth. I often disobeyed orders and dispensed with my mask, partly because I felt stifled with my nose and mouth covered, and partly because my smile helped in this difficult work with difficult people. (Months later at home, when I grew too weak to get out of bed, and coughed blood, dread symptom, and X-rays revealed a shadow on the lungs, first sign of TB, I looked back on those days of idiotic, uncalled-for faith with bemusement. I then had a sense of inviolability, common to children and puppies, a half-conscious sense that Providence would protect the simple-hearted – and the foolish.)

The actual work dispelled any vestigial illusions of the glamor of being a "Flit on, cheering angel" Florence Nightingale of light and mercy. It was "hands-on," occasionally repellent. I often forced myself through the chores by sheer will-power. I reminded myself that I had decided to imitate Christ, and to be a saint in the tradition of Francis of Assisi, Damien, Schweitzer, and Dooley as I fought nausea and changed sheets fouled by the "rice water" stools of cholera patients, the blood and mucus filled feces of those with dysentery.

Why do you do it? Monica, an intense, curly-headed West German volunteer, an atheist, asked. No one assigned me this chore. (On the contrary, as one of the better-educated sisters, I was given the more "prestigious" jobs which required some expertise: to give the patients their daily medication and injections, to set up and administer an intravenous drip when a patient was admitted delirious with typhoid, or with the cold, withered skin, sunken eyes, and icy hands of the cholera victim.) No, I chose. I was struck by the paradigm of Christ, "who, though he was rich, yet he became poor." Born amid a stable's dung, as literally as we cleaned feces; homeless during his ministry; dying naked on the cross. *Come follow me.* "One must go down, as low down as possible to find God," I reasoned with an eighteen-year-old's intensity. And what did I equate "God" with? Joy. Certainty. Peace.

"Oh the mind, mind has mountains." The romance of the spiritual life, its Pilgrim's Progress through internal hills and valleys, shed a gleam on everyday chores – washing clothes or windows, or scrubbing the stainless steel plates left pyramided on the courtyard floor after the patients' evening meal. We hoisted up our sarees hoydenishly and squatted on our haunches to scrub the endless pile of plates with our scourer, a piece of coconut husk, and our home-mixed detergent, ashes and shavings of soap. Western volunteers helped, professing amazement at our primitive methods of washing clothes and dishes. "Mother Teresa has been offered dishwashers and washing machines many times and has refused," I'd say. Mother says that we should live just like the poorest of the poor to be able to understand them," I'd parrot this explanation, smugly and self-righteously – repressing my annoyance at her rigidity on the many days that I was exhausted.

The new admission was brought in on a stretcher – a young girl with a prematurely haggard face, her hair an uncombed, matted mass that I could see we'd have to cut off. How to unravel it? When I undressed her for a sponge bath, I saw that her thighs were blood-stained. Her vulva was a raw, feces-encrusted sore. I involuntarily moved back at the stench. A group of men had slashed her crotch with blades, she said.

"Why did they do that?" I asked, ignorant of perversion. I gathered from her faltering reply in Bengali that she had been forced into prostitution, and that there were all sorts...

"How old are you?"

"Eighteen."

She was my age. I stood, staring at the pus, feces, blood, and raw flesh, wondering what to do first, when Sister Luke appeared. She pushed me aside, her long serious face grim. "Go away, child, go away," she growled, as she bent her lanky body down to the patient, sponging her down with lightening speed. Sister Luke later explained that the girl had venereal disease, something I'd never encountered before.

Sister Luke was good-hearted, but her volatile temper and gruff, no-nonsense manners scared patients, postulants, and volunteers alike. My parents, visiting, were shocked and upset to hear her scream at the patients. Indeed, her manner was far from the ideal for workers in the Home for the Destitute that Mother Teresa recommends in the Constitution: *Death, sacred to all men, is the final stage of complete development on this earth. Having lived well, we wish for ourselves and for all men to die beautifully. We train ourselves to be extremely kind and gentle in touch of hand, tone of voice, and in our smile so as to make the mercy of God very real and to induce the dying person to turn to God with filial confidence.*

Sister Luke, a trained nurse, entrusted me with deciphering the doctor's scribbled prescriptions, and doling out the evening medication; I'd had more education than most novices. I also gave the injections and intravenous drips when I came on duty. In the absence of professionals, we picked up the elements of nursing from one another. I am sometimes appalled, remembering our amateurishness, but then recall that we looked after people we carried in from the streets, whom no one else cared about, and that we did alleviate their pain.

One evening, I balanced a tray of medicine – Chloramphenicol, Ampicillin, Streptomycin, isoniazid – sorted out in little cups, in one hand as I left the office to begin my rounds. I tripped. Hundreds of pink, white, and parti-colored pills raced over the floor. Sister Luke had locked the medicine cupboard. Too terrified to ask her for a fresh dose for the hundred and twenty patients, I began to pick the pills off the floor, intending to use them anyway. The colored or unusually shaped pills were easy to separate. I slowed down at the homogenized mass of white pills, a desperate Psyche, fond hope and guesswork intermingling as I sorted, when Nemesis descended.

"What *are* you doing?" Sister Luke stood over me, her hands on her hips.

I told her.

"You blessed child. You stupid child," she shrieked, throwing the tray into the trash, cups and all, tossing me her keys to get a fresh dose.

Sister Luke had probably sworn freely before she became a nun. Perhaps her favorite swearword had been the Anglo-Indian "bloody." Now, she had ingeniously transmuted worldly expletives into heavenly ones. "Get the blessed bedpan to that blessed patient," she'd scream. Sister Luke was admired, almost hero-worshiped, by all who worked in Kalighat – she was dedicated, efficient and unpretentious – so "Blessed" became a common expletive for all "Lukies."

For the first few weeks, I scrupulously followed the doctor's charts as I gave the patients their medication. But as the medicine and dosages grew familiar, I began to trust my memory. Teachers and friends had often commented on my "photographic memory," and I was proud of it. I made a point of smiling at Krishna, an emaciated pale-faced teenager with close-cropped hair, as I gave her her medicine. ("Smile five times a day at people you do not feel like smiling at. Do it for world peace," Mother Teresa said. I'd cheat though, selecting targets whom I liked, at least a little.)

Too frail to sit up, Krishna lay on propped-up pillows, a faint smile on her face, her eyes huge and haunted. She looked classically tubercular, like Severn's portrait of the dying Keats.

One evening, Krishna shivered feverishly, face flushed, eyes streaming. Her forehead burned. I studied the thermometer: a hundred and six, the highest I'd recorded.

I went to Sister Luke. "Sister, the girl with TB has a very high temperature," I said.

"Which girl?"

"Krishna."

"Krishna!" She laughed. "You know, Krishna was severely malnourished when she was brought to us. She looked as gaunt as a TB patient. We thought she was going to die. But she is recovering nicely. I think we will be able to discharge her soon.. You say she is sick?"

Malnutrition! I flushed. Krishna was not sick. She had starved. And I had given her the dosage of Isoniazid for a severely tubercular patient. I had been cautioned never to dispense these pills carelessly.

"Krishna is feverish," I mumbled, and slunk away, stunned, too cowardly to tell her what I'd done. *If I have to confess, I will, but please, oh God, oh God, heal her.*

A Calcutta volunteer doctor was at work. I feigned jocularity. "So Doctor, what happens if you take drugs for TB when you don't have TB?"

"You want to kill yourself, Sister? You could pop off. That's potent stuff."

I had guessed that already; why did I ask? Miserable, remorseful about my hubris, I dashed to Krishna's bedside with paracetamol for her fever and laid my hands on the surprised girl's head. "Now Krishna, listen. You are not feeling well, right? I'm going to pray for you. Right now." I prayed desperately, imploring for her life.

No result. I had other duties, but every few minutes, I stole to Krishna's bedside, praying for her, for a miracle. Gradually Krishna's fever subsided, her temperature returned to normal, though she was very weak.

I felt close to Krishna after all this. The severely malnourished girl had grown too weak to walk. And since she lay all day on her jute-strung cot, her legs atrophied. As she grew stronger, I helped her to walk again, walking beside her, her arms round my shoulders, or walking in front of her, holding her hands, until she regained balance and confidence and strength.

Krishna walked, shakily but unaided, before I left. I saw her discharged, another Lazarus restored, another woman returned to Calcutta's Darwinian struggle for survival, but with an ounce of hope. One drop removed from the ocean of misery – but the ocean would be greater were it there.

5 | Domesticity and Art

It speaks a language of its own, sometimes in such insistent tones that it interrupts the quietness of my own thoughts. At times, my house seems haunted like the castle of fairy tales in which the clock, the teapot, and candelabra whisper secret admonition: "Careful beauty. Here lurks a beast."

When oft upon my couch I lie, in vacant or in pensive mood... No such luck in my house, not for long. It chatters. It nags me. "Mop those spills," shrills the kitchen floor. "Observe the smudge where you've done aerobics," the carpet nudges in urgent tongues; "use Resolve." And the blob on the bannister where Zoe's peanut butter and jelly hugs hair and dust reproaches me like her jammy baby face – "*bad mother, bad housewife, bad.*" My house admonishes me – as demanding as a mother or toddler – so much so that I flee it for tranquility, taking ill-earned vacations in Japan, Israel, Holland, New Zealand, the ends of the earth.

Though it often radiates serenity. I like to walk around my home – bright and airy. The garden and the woods spill in through the skylights, the picture windows, the French doors. In the evening hours when the light from the Tiffany lamp burns a deeper red on the burgundy carpet, and the quick beams of the hanging brass lamp from India dart sapphire and amber, ruby and emerald, echoing the smoldering stained glass windows; and the house and everything bright and beautiful in it glows like a chapel at dusk – I fairly purr with contentment. This beauty I have assembled, no, created, if making a collage is creation.

Then the house seems a mosaic of the life my husband Roy and I have created together, our taste and our past, our passion for art, the countries we've lived and traveled in, our friends, their gifts.

"Every man is the builder of a temple called his body to the god he worships," Thoreau says. How much easier to make your house a museum of your ideals and passions! For without the sweat and bother of calculating minutes or calories or grams, you can create – within the limits of time, money and imagination – beauty, "that superfluous, that necessary thing."

In this, our ninth year of marriage, I often look around and think – *yours*, before we got married; *mine*, before...(increasingly fewer since we upgrade when time or money show up, striving to fill our home with beauty) and *ours* – the handwoven silk carpet from Kashmir, its vines and flowers a tangle of tendrils; or the glass paperweight from Cambridge, England, with entrapped royal blue crocuses, the color of tropical skies at dusk, yellow flames at their deep hearts. Gifts leap out, dissonances in our taste – the clock from 50,000 year old Kauri wood from New Zealand given by Roy's parents, with a too gleaming lacquer; the ponderous, antique Chinese monarchs carved, with delicate filigree tracery, from walrus tusks, given by my parents. And in this mellow mood, which calls for Grand Marnier or Drambuie, everything in the mosaic speaks of love – difficult, tentative love. Oh forget love, vague, overused word; let's say goodwill. I sit on our Queen Anne couch, its lush upholstery the color of a "vintage that hath been cooled a long age in the deep-delved earth, tasting of Flora and the country green, dance and Provencal song, and sunburnt mirth" and bask in the bright color, savoring a brief interlude of harmony.

What most depresses me about the work of houses is that it is not linear, but cyclical. You may never step into the same river twice, but you step, so to say, into the same dishes twice, the same rugs, the same laundry. Nothing can rescue you from them, not virtue, wisdom, time management, or the seven secrets of highly effective people. I like linear things. "If one advances confidently in the direction of his dreams and endeavors to live the life which he has imagined, he will meet a success undreamed of in lesser hours," Thoreau declares. Emerson says, "No matter where you begin, read anything for five hours a day and you will soon be knowing." (*Five hours a day to read!* I had them once.) You work at writing for two hours a day, or, better still, four (*four* hours?) and begin to forge a style. Bring up a child wisely and lovingly, and you will eventually have an new friend, fascinating to you. But in the eternal circularity of housework, you joust with the same house, seared, bleared, smeared day after day, battle the same smells and smudges. Fiddly little things. Fingerprints on the mirror, a raisin trodden into the hardwood floor. Ignore them at your peril. They peck at your spirit, inanimate petitioners, presenting their mute To Do list each time your eyes fall on them. And time, life, leaks away.

The best way to deal with housework is the way they advised us in school to study for exams. Everyday, throughout the year, a little at a time. Like weeding – little and often. But, as Parkinson's law drearily predicts, housework expands all the available time . There's always more – dusting baseboards, washing windows, organizing closets. I think of Coleridge's lament, "Work without hope draws nectar in a sieve."

Metaphors in Greek mythology illuminate housework – spectral soldiers that sprang from the slain dragon's teeth, and each bone of each slain soldier sprouted a fresh army; the heads of the hydra; Sisyphus hefting that stone up the hill only to have it rumble down again; or mint! The nymph Minthe was discovered in the arms of Pluto by his wife Persephone, who crushed the little creature savagely underfoot. Pluto metamorphosed her into mint which, in response to pruning, sends out new growth, that rascally herb, except that I cannot have too much of herbs. I use them for tea and fragrant baths and pestos; in bouquets and winter fires and occasionally – risky this – as medicine.

Sartre said he wanted to know more than anyone else in the world which explained the state of his room. But I feel the dissonance of making beautiful art surrounded by disorder and squalor. In fact, cleaning my house often feels like a creative act, restoring it to quietness, conjuring (like a Michaelangelesque deity) order from the chaos it degenerates into in the periods – the time out of time – when I live in my head, and nothing is more real than the book I am absorbed in reading, or the essay I am lost in writing.

Our rules are the strings of a kite, explained the Principal of St. Mary's Convent, my strict Catholic boarding school in the Himalayas. Their strictures steady you, help you fly. My house is what those rules were claimed to be: a scaffolding, an exoskeleton. I crumble when I rebel against its carapace, the demands of a balanced life – making time not just for reading and writing, but also for playing and reading with my daughters; for exercise; prayer and Scripture; housework; and for my hour of gardening which is family time, meditation, and therapy rolled into one. For reading and writing can colonize, take over a life. I overwork, I grow exhausted. During my four residencies at idyllic artists' colonies, where all I had to do was read and write, I often felt writeen out and restless, whereas within the narrow channels of my old life, I was a limpid stream. Having only an hour or two to write in – like knowing you will be executed in the morning – concentrates the mind. The freedom at the colony, those long hours to read and write amid the river of molten silver, the waterfalls, the covered bridges, the green mountains, in fact make me feel disoriented and depressed. I missed the carnival of our fast-paced family life and my high-spirited toddler. Depression, the specter at the feast, stalks days set apart for pleasure – birthdays, Christmas, a week in Paris. Joy comes unsought like the bluebird that surprises us at our feeder. Hunted, it is elusive.

I used to attend a writers' conference a year when I first started writing – waited tables at Bread Loaf, went to Mount Holyoke, Wesleyan, Chenango Valley...wherever I got a scholarship. And I'd go home in a mania of resolution, full of decisions to revise my life, with lists of books to be read, essays to be written, followed by a memoirs, historical or biographical creative nonfiction, who knows what, Catherine Wheels of excitement in my head. And then – life. Distraction. A toddler, housework, marriage, friends, dinner parties, mail, the telephone, tiredness. And the dream of creating exquisite literature can grow more tenuous until it becomes a secret garden to retreat to and dream. If only...some day...when – more hours, more money, more energy, no child, no spouse, no housework, no house, no life... But no, art must bloom – we must let it – quiet and determined in the cracks of time left us by the vexations of life, like saxifrage, tiny blue flower that splits rocks.

And if an hour is all our brimming lives offer us to write, we write for but an hour. An hour was the most I had in the months I raised my infant daughter, Zoe, as puzzled as that duck rearing a cygnet. She seemed of another species, kittenlike, puppyish, so mysterious her cries. She was tiny, six pounds, twelve ounces, and fragile. Her head had to be supported like an antique doll's. Her arms and legs were spindly. "She's smaller than a doll-baby!" children said. Her lips were as perfectly contoured as a rosebud; her eyes large and gray, then later hazel; her fingers long and sensitive – an artist's fingers, people said; a pianist's. A gynecologist's, I said, who had just had my cervix checked in a most old-fashioned way in an otherwise high-tech pregnancy.

How magical and downy is a creature straight from the womb, how small. I could not sleep near her. I thought of the harlot in the Book of Kings who rolled over her sleeping baby and killed him. I could not sleep away from her. I wondered if she had cried for me until she had choked on her tears and throw-up, and had died of exhaustion and a broken heart. I rushed to her crib. I could not sleep. Death and disaster seemed to threaten her on every side – the stairs, electric sockets, cleaning supplies under the sink, the telephone ringing while she was on the changing table, the stove, the iron, my rambunctious dog, the neighbor's cat who I've heard might lie on a newborn's chest attracted by its sweet, milky breath, and suck the life out of it – and then malign visitants like SIDS. If she slept unusually long, I raced to her in terror, placing my face against hers to hear, to feel her breathe, and, of course, she woke, crying, and that was it for writing for that morning, that afternoon. For the eighteen overwrought months that I looked after her full time, I held my breath. I didn't exhale and, of course, I didn't write, except for bittersweet journals full of the wonder of Zoe, but also of despair at "that one talent which is death to hide, lodged with me useless" – frustration and sadness mixed with an almost physical, passionate, longing love of my daughter, journals I cannot read today. It's painful.

Two years, three months (and some green and white pills) after the birth of Zoe, I made peace with my life. If I were to choose a figure from mythology as inspiration and hope, it would not be Apollo, Sun God of music and poetry, bright and free, uncaring about babies, diapers, or better homes and gardens he, but Antaeus, whom I imagine as massive, bowed, like Rodin's "Thinker." And when enemy pressure forced him to the earth, from the earth he drew strength, and energy from failure.

To distill art from my daily life. Before Zoe came, I considered writing about the Mughal dynasty of India – Babar, Humayun, Akbar, who invented a religion of his own, Din-i-ilahi, divine light, a melange of every religion he knew; Shah Jahan, esthete, who had the Taj Mahal carved in memory of his beloved dead wife, Mumtaz; and Aurungzeb, his son, religious fanatic who hated the father who best loved his older brother, and ultimately killed them both. I wanted to write too, fiction or "creative nonfiction," of the Pre-Raphaelites, delirious with youth and golden dreams, painting murals on the walls of the Oxford Union, not caring if they would last; or Milton, the master poet who decided "to justify the ways of God to man," stoic, disciplined, admirable in his high-minded misery. The austere blind poet, in his study each morning, a canto of Paradise Lost in his head, waiting to be "milked."

Now the catalyst for my essays could be houses, gardens, babies, busyness, domesticity. My daily life provides inspiration and material, which is just as well, for, at present, I lack much time or energy to rummage in the second-hand gift shop of Art or other people's lives. "Write about what your everyday life offers you," Rilke says in his heartening Letters to a Young Poet. "And if your everyday life seems poor, don't blame it, blame yourself; admit to yourself that you are not enough of a poet to call forth its riches," to (segueing into another visionary) "see a world in a grain of sand, and a heaven in a wild flower, hold infinity in the palm of your hand, and eternity in an hour."

You can almost hear the silence. The milkmaid serenely fills her earthenware bowl. "The Young Woman with a Jug" pauses to dream out of the window. The lacemaker is lost in her work. I gaze at Vermeer's women. I trust most things that help me lose track of time – reading, writing, gardening, hiking, the sea, art galleries, prayer, sex, good movies, good conversation. Vermeer's women lose themselves is: housework. It glows! Is this domesticity? Can it be? That's the way I want to live my life, like "Woman Holding a Balance," slowly, tranquilly, not fighting the irrelevant relevant, the distracting, trivial and necessary tasks of my days, but embracing them as an oasis of contemplation in which desert flowers may bloom.

Vermeer's paintings, poems one might say, on the radiance of domesticity are more moving when we learn of the hurly-burly of his household – a wife, eleven children, and a feisty mother-in-law. Those paintings that could have been called "Shanti, shanti, shanti" or "Tranquility" instead of "Girl Reading a Letter at an Open Window" are probably sighs of yearning, images of an elusive Eden. They hint how manual work – if used as time for contemplation – might be redeemed, the chores we all have in an egalitarian society, save those with a somewhat rarefied life, like the wife of a college president, who told me she gets her laundry done – even your lingerie and nightclothes? I asked; everything, she said – and, what's more, picked up off the bedroom floor; her silver polished and porcelain dusted; her flowers arranged; and meals cooked and served and cleaned up by the staff of the President's House. Or people with illegal immigrant maids. And they don't really have more free time; they are as busy as the rest of us. For work encroaches on their chore time, time to catch one's breath and think – if we live calmly, creatively – with a touch of Old World realism, the acceptance of inevitable imperfection. To fight the trivial that sprouts in its insistent dandelion way around the intense, focussed life we strive for, is to saturate what could have been the fruitful soil of our lives with resentment, making of it a sad burden. How much better to live as Vermeer's women, and use distraction, housework, as a salt lick, a breathing space, the clearing in the forest for pixie thought to dance.

In Vermeer's "Christ in the House of Martha and Mary" Mary sat at the Lord's feet, listening to what he said" while "Martha was distracted by all the preparations that had to be made." Jesus responds to Martha's complaints, "Martha, Martha, you are worried and upset about many things, but only one thing is needed. Mary has chosen what is better." Poor Martha. What a put-down for domesticity. Though I identify with Mary, for I too, given the presence of Martha, would have sat rapt at Jesus' feet, detached from the domestic hurly-burly. Traditionally, Mary represents otium sanctum, "holy leisure," the contemplative life while Martha represents the active life. "You write about houses; I work on our house!" – a postscript to the fax my husband sends me at the Vermont Studio Center, an artists' colony. I draft this essay on domesticity while he halts his mathematical research to rewax our tile floors, refinish our hardwood floors, repaint our walls and decks.

I read his faxes on the baroque process of refinishing hardwood floors – five sandings with a belt sander until the floor was as smooth as a baby; the staining with two coats of Golden Maple; the spraying with four coats of polyurethane. Your sweat-equity makes your house gleam for you, I muse, makes it your own, like a hand-knitted sweater, fruit of time, labor, and attention. It's like marrying a man, adopting a dog, creating a baby. You love them because you chose them, bought them, bore them. But what makes them more precious to you is the time you've invested in them – the hours you have spent with your daughter so that her chatter is predictable, and yet amusing. Or the long years with your husband, which makes his habit of thinking the best of the most incorrigible rascals; his naivete as he swallows your imaginative fictions; his sense of humor, his laughter, beloved – even his occasional, almost comic despondency at the intractability of his wife and child and life.

Marriage should be a true communist state: from each according to his ability to each according to her need, I fax Roy back. And Roy is the mathematician, gifted with numbers and with the esoteric facets of money, but also skilled with his hands, strong. My hands fly on a computer keyboard – "the pooter," Zoe calls her rival – but they falter at detail work. I can, though, imagine the elegant and beautiful in photographic detail. So we have achieved "a winning combination" (so I say; Roy's ambivalent) where I conceive of the enchanting room, the Edenic garden, and Roy executes it, making curtains, and mantelpieces, and bogs to grow cranberries. Though both of us would rather be the brain, and not the hands – unless those hands are on the keyboard. "There are three brains in this house," Roy says, exasperated, "but only one pair of hands. And that is the problem."

How holy is work in Vermeer's art. I remember seeing – on long bus trips from Delhi up to my boarding school in Nainital in the Himalayas – "Work is worship" splashed white on the rocks of the hillsides by the sort of man with a mission who spray-paints "Jesus Saves" on bridges across America – a hit and run operation. I wonder if the Catholic Vermeer knew of the old Benedictine ideal, Laborare est orare, work is prayer. Surely. I like the idea – all of life, sacred, to rejoice in, whether we work with our hands or pens or paintbrushes; or love and play and pray. As I wash my windows, I sing, lyrical hymns, and my spirit soars. He who sings prays two-fold, Augustine declared; the melody provides an updraft to the emotion of worship. The work of writing absorbs all your attention like a stained glass window. But domestic work is a clear pane of glass, through which the spirit wings. I am enveloped in stillness – even joy – while my hands clean.

I tidy my study, working around the trampoline where my daughter Zoe sits cross-legged, spellbound by the cheery domesticity in Snow White. Zoe, at three, refuses to be in any room except the one where her mummy is; she often sleeps on my side of the bed. Cinderella waltzes with her broom. Snow White sings as she scrubs. How effortless these Disney heroines make labor seem. Laborare est orarare, work is prayer; but more – work can be joy. I tend to do my housework slowly, dreamily shining the antique silver I've inherited before a dinner party, while minutes. Housework is a form of settling down, organizing and clarifying my thoughts, no less than my house. If you do them contemplatively, I've discovered, domestic chores can be bursts of grace, time to slow down and praise the beauty of the day, the trees outside the window: disguised leisure to think. I am absorbed in the rosary of work until it fades away, becomes mechanical, while "the mind from pleasure less, withdraws into its happiness."

"Are you dreaming?" my husband comes upon me, startling me. I have been shining my grandmother's silver filigreed salver for – I don't know – five minutes, ten? Yes, I say sheepishly. I'd lost track of time. The guests will be here in thirty minutes and I have but half our formal living room room cleaned – not just cleaned but sparkling, the silver shined, the brass buffed, but in the kitchen, spills on the linoleum, and Zoe's stuff sprawls over the family room. "Prioritize," my husband says, "Prioritize." And he whisks through the house, mopping counters, sinks, floors, bathrooms. Roy's faster than that cleaning lady famous in Williamsburg, who cleans a house in forty-five minutes, and charges as much as a psychiatrist, and for whom there is a waiting list – and as our first guests ready their smiles at the doorbell, wondrously, our house is ready too.

I hope the guests won't notice any holdouts of dust and dirt, and, of course, they don't seem to. One of the lessons my house has taught me: No one knows your house as you do. So no one sees the flaws you see. The spots, the cracks beneath its sheen never jar another as they jar you. The artist obsesses about the dragonfly-winged columbine she's painted crooked in a corner; the viewer blinks, dazzled at the canvas on the wall.

I visited the Daffodil Festival at Gloucester, Virginia, an arts and crafts fair, with friends from church: an accountant, an engineer, a hospital administrator; superwomen who wake at five and exercise, earn good money, have beautiful homes and bouncy children. Susan asked us what we would do if we were to choose, once again, a career. I said I might be a Christian psychotherapist. The zigzag to maturity, occasionally assisted by therapy, has been for me a process of transforming cognitive leaps – and of spiritual leaps. Immersing myself in the Gospel accounts of Jesus, that wise, entirely original God/man, studying Jesus, trying to live his teachings within the perimeters of my life as a writer, mom and faculty wife in suburban America and – ah – my courage is gradually changing me. I cannot fathom the chaos if I chose another way to live.

Anyway, the others decided they would be – no, not stay-at-home moms as punitive misogynistic moralists might surmise, but – interior decorators. Interior Decorators! They detailed a creative life as we walked: buying houses, furnishing and decorating them, exhibiting them in the Southern Parade of Homes, and then selling them – to embark on the whole process again. Huh!

Had I missed something? I avoid opening those glossy magazines in the optometrist's office, fearing the wave of restlessness, followed by the next wave of time-consuming, money-devouring ideas. I've felt covetousness and desire germinate as I looked at Better Homes and Gardens, or as an impoverished professor we know mourns, "Better Homes Than Yours" and swiftly closed it. I have neither time nor money to squander, I told myself severely. But I did buy a book on interior decoration.

Buddha would have laughed at the thing, the Buddha who, attaining enlightenment after his sojourn under the Bodhi tree, formulated his Four Noble Truths: Life is suffering; Suffering originates from our desire for pleasure; Suffering can be eliminated by destroying desire; desire is eliminated by the noble eight-fold path of right belief, aspirations, livelihood, mindfulness, speech, conduct, exertion, and meditation. That's too quietest, and self-protective a way for me. Perhaps, you can avoid suffering by avoiding desire. but I don't want to live like that. I want to live intensely, flinging myself into experience, and not hold back because my heart might be broken. Let it! The heartbreak does not neutralize the glimpse of "splendor in the grass, of glory in the flower."

Would Jesus have looked at my book on interior decoration, Jesus with his compassionate interest in everything, everyone – prostitutes, demoniacs, blind men, tax collectors, and lepers – that leapt past social constraints, his loving outward gaze? To think of him is to introduce a lighthouse's pulsar of luminosity into turbulence. What a great writer he could have been, with his kind and penetrating eyes; his gentleness, wisdom, and shrewdness! But he did greater things, illuminating the counter-intuitive surprising paths to joy. He who seeks to save his life shall lose it, and he who loses his life for my sake shall save it. Unless a grain of wheat falls into the earth and dies it remains alone, but if it dies it yields a mighty harvest. In the largesse of self you receive – fruitfulness, joy. Though not a word he wrote survives, his words and life still blaze. Jesus may well have looked, if he had the leisure. But what would he have said?

He himself dispensed with a house during his intense, dramatic three years of public life when he was, strictly speaking, homeless. I study the gospels each morning; in the tired evening, I occasionally leaf through the catalogs that, through the machinations of omniscient computers, heap my mailbox – Winterthur, Toscano, Earthly Treasures, the lifestyles of the rich and frazzled. And I hear his quiet voice caution, "Beware of covetousness. Watch out! Be on your guard against all kinds of greed; a man's life does not consist in the abundance of his possessions."

As I leaf through my new books on the Arts and Crafts Movement, the aesthetic I feel the most kinship with, I call Roy over to look at beautiful and austere furniture, carpets, lamps, vases, tapestries – art that works, art that's part of life. His nose wrinkles. "Get rid of those books," Roy exhorts me. "Immediately. They will waste our time, add to our possessions, more stuff to maintain. But – if you donate them to the library, we get a tax deduction!" But what about making the home you live in a haven of beauty? I argue. A cool magical peaceful space, like a museum. Surely if you do it in your spare hours – if it comes second to forming a beautiful spirit, child, book, or life – it's not a trivial pursuit, I maintain, uncertainly. (Spare hours?) I read out the recommendation of Dr. Andrew Weil (the alternative medicine guru I consult as I recover from anachronistic complications after a miscarriage, and a man of good sense, whose simple advice actually works – not true which of every best-selling dreamer who promises an ageless body on an impossible diet!). It's imperative, the good doctor declares, for those who dwell in cities to make their home "a place of serenity, beauty, and order...a quiet place to relax."

I consider creation – from the delicacy of the deep purple Dutch iris, its yellow tongue a flaming invitation to pollinators, to the colony of seals flippering on the pancake rocks, where the sea surges through blowholes in the South Island of New Zealand with its glowworm caves, rain forests, glaciers, and icy mountain tarns – all encountered in a day's drive. The world: So various, so beautiful, so new, fickle, freckled, (who knows how?) Our homes should reflect some of nature's loveliness – or am I rationalizing? How much? Wisdom probably lies in Aristotle's golden mean between extremes: in this case, between the drably functional, and a cold pursuit of beauty that ignores those for whom beauty would be a blanket, a meal, a shack of their own. How do we, practically, find a balance between sipping the richness of life, and retaining compassion for others without which beauty can turn to ugliness of spirit – a wilted wild flower, a mangled butterfly, the manna of the ancient Israelites in the desert which, when hoarded, rotted and wriggled with worms? I myself, pretty much since I've had any money to speak of, have followed the ancient practice of tithing – giving away ten percent of one's income to "the wretched of the earth" – recommended in "that nice clever book," the Bible (as my naturally religious three-year old Zoe, an anima naturalater Christianita, calls it; "That cutie Jesus," she amusingly says). It is a clever idea, easy to calculate; and since each possession devours time – acquiring, dusting, repairing, fretting – in giving, you receive time and space and an increased immunity to the siren song of money, tricky substance: life-enhancing if you use it lightly, creatively, or share it; sterile, Midasian, yet addictive if it's hoarded (which is substance abuse). A good servant, but a bad master – like coffee, melatonin, or red wine.

Oh no! For all their warm fuzzy connotations – family values; one's secret castle; enchanted island – talk of houses inevitably snakes to the murky, socially taboo subject of money which artists are meant to disdain, and which, like sex, one can more or less do without – for a time – but it's rough. Our two great areas of secret curiosity about our acquaintance: sex and money, how much, and how, and with how much sweat or fun. It takes, among other things, money (or leisure, the fruit of money) to produce beauty or art – a crass truth, like Jamaica Kincaid's observation that it takes wealth to create a Paradisial garden, a universal truth rarely acknowledged. And yet, and yet, how many of humankind's heroes have shed this bourgeois stuff – the Buddha, Socrates, Jesus, Francis of Assisi, Thoreau, Mahatma Gandhi... They tramped ill-clothed, ill-fed, ill-housed and free, with little, and little to worry about. It's like the Pegasus wings you sprout when you reduce your life to a suitcase and go traveling – with its burst of new ideas and its enlarged perspective.

The radiant Walden was conceived in Thoreau's shed of a cabin – his flamboyant symbol of the simple life! Simplify, simplify, he says, oppressor – but when I consider beauty made by human hands, whether the mosaics in the Dome of the Rock in Jerusalem, the stained glass rose windows of Notre Dame de Paris, or the sweetest perfumes, a blend of high, middle and low notes, I realize an antiphonic retort also serves as a definition for beauty: complicate, complicate. For beauty, whether in art, interior decoration, or a life, is a montage of simplicity and complexity, just as delicious prose is a symphony of long sentences and short, the long transporting us with verbal loveliness; the short, startling us, enforcing attention. No more lotus-eating luxuriance. Now think.

Our houses are the ornate tortoise shells we haul. For though dead cells like nails or hair – or the shells of abalone or coral – they are part of us, an extension of us. At times, we stagger beneath the sheer heft of them, but at other times, the intricacy of their carapace lends vibrance to our lives. I would feel restless in Thoreau's cabin, and crave color, a subdued classical elegance. I often think of the sheer beauty of the Italian Gothic interior of the Church of Santa Maria Novella in Florence, and of Giotto's campanile a short walk away! I want everything in my house to be both beautiful and useful, I decided even before I heard of Ruskin's exhilarating aesthetic. I was charmed by Japanese homes, the austere decoration which breathed quietness. Instead of the clutter of bric-a-brac, the necessary mirrors, tissue boxes, paper knives, carved, engraved, inlaid, were art. We brought back a black lacquer tray on which a spare maple wept gold leaves into a gold stream, onto a single gold rock, the Zen focal point for walking meditations. On our return, I decided to gradually exchange each of the necessary objects in my house for beautiful ones, adding pottery bowls the color of lapis lazuli that smoke out a wisp of pleasure each time I look at them; salt and pepper shakers, with spirals of brown, deep red and orange, made from the burnished heartwood of Rosewood, Dalberga, from Brazil; and pottery planters, with wild iridescent sweeps of amethyst and azure for our indoor garden of bananas, tangerine, cardamom and bay trees – beauty without the jostle of additional possessions.

I resolve my ambivalence. For an hour or so a day, I organize my house, trying to make it exquisite, bright, surprising, tranquil. A room, a home, reflects one's spirit. They are an outward sign of inward grace or turbulence. So I hope, in reverse, that to create a home that could be called La Serenissima, most serene, will entice its sweetness to steal over you. Of late, two of the things I pour extra money into, when I have it, are travel (ah, the hassles of home!) and (ah, the hassles of travel!) my home, trying to create within it, beauty. "Will we soon have guided tours to the Mathias Art Gallery, Garden and Library?" Roy enquires. I love those houses converted to art galleries – the Frick, the Phillips, and, especially, the Isabella Gardner with its headstrong eclecticism, kitsch and Vermeer cohabiting, Mrs. Gardner's sensibility the only apparent aesthetic. My other favorite, the Huntington Library, Art Gallery and Botanical Garden in Pasadena, a collector's garden with 207 acres of the flora of every practicable climate zone, evokes in me deep pleasure, not without a restless desire for emulation. We attempted "edible landscaping," converting our suburban lawn, backyard, and wooded lot in Williamsburg, Virginia into an orchard of exotic fruit trees and bushes; planting dozens of herbs, the only thing I collect; and every flower we have room to grow that the herds of deer that haunt Kingmill, our wooded community on the James River, turn up their dainty noses at.

The true cost of things, Thoreau wrote, is the "life" it takes to earn the money to buy them. I look around me. Life leaking into the perfection of crystal water pitchers, or the vase from Japan handpainted with the understated elegance of purple irises, my favorite flower, a motif in our home and garden. Whoa! But how was that money – that, according to Thoreau, represents life – acquired? That is the question. Mine, by playing with words and ideas; my husband's – ah! – by researching the arcana of mathematics which he enjoys. (Does this sound vague? So is my understanding of his work. "How do you research mathematics?" people ask, or "Can you explain your research to me in terms a layperson would understand?" Then I switch off, as I suspect, do they.) The trade-off of leisure for beauty one enjoys daily was not a ridiculous exchange my husband decided, as he resolved that, if we eventually needed the money, he'd teach his favorite courses some summer so we could, without guilt, buy in Florence the antique black Belgian marble chest inlaid with sixty semiprecious stones in the Medici tradition of pietre dure, their names like a magical chant out of Revelation – malachite, rhodocrosyte, chalcedony, lapis lazuli, jasper, jade, onyx, moonstone, tiger eye, falcon eye... In Venice, Roy succumbed to a monumental paperweight, a collector's treasure, which had trapped in heavy glass, floating as in a sea, the millefiori, the thousand iridescent flowers of Murano glass, each a brilliant mosaic of many more, that intricate loveliness a master craftsman's work. "I guess I'm a sucker for beauty," he sighed.

And I? I would not directly trade leisure for beauty – or work a job other than writing to acquire the most bellissimo object. Though I do happily exchange money my essays earn in the feast or famine way of art, for work of other artists that captivates me with its loveliness – such as my bowl of woven glass, the variegated, jewelly ribbons of violet, crimson, magenta, maroon and purple crisscrossed with sudden surprise strands of pink, blue, white, and black. And if my writing cannot be exchanged for money – a risk you take when you follow your bliss in creative work? Well, I would still have beautiful things I've slowly made, with my hands on the keyboard, work I'm proud of, like an old-fashioned craftsman.

My work is like Thoreau's: reading, research into life, writing up conclusions. This he considered the noblest work, the work that alone was life. To work jobs to earn money to buy things was to trade life for things. In his Thorovian arrogance, however, he assumed that an architect, a mathematician, a carpenter, a gardener could not enjoy their work as much as he enjoyed his, and, therefore, happily exchange the fruit of work they loved to acquire things they loved. For him, work was tainted by Adam's curse to painful, sweaty toil. "Trade curses everything it handles; and though you trade in messages from heaven, the whole curse of trade attaches to the business," he wrote. So he tried to narrow "work" (growing beans) to six weeks a year to "live" (read and write) for the rest of it. But how blessed not to be at war with half your life, to be able to unite "vocation and avocation, as the two eyes make one in sight," to consider all your life – making money, housekeeping, reading, writing, friendships, gardening, thinking – as your work; and all your work – beans and books – as your life.

I considered intellectual work sacred, a sea to slough grief. In my twenties, the Thorovian conflict of work and life was won, overwhelmingly, by "work" – reading and study, though I have never worked a "regular" job, having quit my Ph.D program to stay home, and write, read, and nurture children. I am beginning, in my ninth year as a more or less stay-at-home woman, to consider it all one. I no longer mind domestic work if there is not too much, nor too much pressure, if I can tackle chores dreamily after a bout of intellectual and creative work. Domestic work is then a way of relaxation, of rumination. I think while I work in my house or garden; I think and record while I write. It is all one. I remember stress rising when, as an undergraduate studying English at Oxford, and – like almost every other undergraduate studying English there – aspiring to be a writer, I encountered the sweeping statement of Alexander Pope, "Writing well, immortally well, is such as a task as does not leave one time to plant a tree, be a useful friend, much less to save one's soul." Oh no, would I never have a dog?

"The intellect of man is forced to choose, perfection of the life or the work," Yeats lamented. Well, I eschew Willa Cather's "God of art that demands human sacrifices." Perfection of the art from a cramped, narrow life? No, a too intensely focused life cramps the omnivorous interests, the broad experience and empathy which provide the sinews of great art. So: a full life and excellent art, if not perfect art. That's enough for me. Art need not be perfectly perfect – as Mona Lisa, Venus de Milo or Diana, Princess of Wales are great beauties, not perfect ones. You grow the best art you can in the soil of the life you have chosen. Who needs to be Trollope and write seventy books? Who reads all seventy anyway? Now – mellowed from my anxious, striving twenties into my wry, better-balanced thirties (a great decade!) – I no longer believe that creating good art must come at the expense of the "the last, the greatest art," the good life – or vice versa. I want to make art that is beautiful, rich, wise, interesting. And I wish it to spring from a life that is rich, wise, interesting. A modest proposal: Good art from a good life. I think that's my goal for the remaining sixty four years,

I hope, left to me – to be "busy at home," reading, writing, sending out work, nurturing my children, gardening, having friends visit, creating a home that is beautiful and serene – the nesting instinct, powerful in women as in pigeons, drawing me homewards.

6 | Aliens and Strangers

I have an idea that some men are born out of their due place. Accident has cast them amid strangers in their birthplace, and the leafy lanes they may have known from childhood remain but a place of passage. They may spend their whole lives aliens among their kindred and remain aloof among the only scenes they have ever known. Perhaps it is this sense of strangeness that sends men far and wide in the search for something permanent to which they may attach themselves.

The Moon and Sixpence, W. Somerset Maugham, 1919

Sometimes, unexpectedly, you come to a place where your spirit unfurls; it has found its natural topography. I like Rilke's notion of spiritual homes, "elective homelands," – for him, Russia, Paris, Switzerland. The Pythagorean and Hindu doctrine of metempsychosis, transmigration of the soul, tries to explain such affinities. *Twice or thrice had I loved thee/ Before I knew thy face or name*, John Donne expresses this sensation. Hindus say of a preternaturally wise child: she has an old soul. My daughter Zoe is like that, uncannily wise. Just two, going on three, she advised me when I was infuriated, "Just 'nore him. What matter what he do-es? Jesus loves us, Jesus is everywhere, Jesus can do anything," repeating in a childish fashion – in the reciprocal teaching that is one of the gifts of having children – the old words of Paul I had taught her, "Neither death nor life, neither angels nor demons, neither the present nor the future, nor any powers, neither height nor depth, nor anything else in all creation shall separate us from the love of God."

My happiest childhood experiences were in books, a contained world of peace, sweeter and more nourishing than the real life around me. Most books I read were set in England, Enid Blyton's Noddy and the Famous Four, and Malory Towers, and St. Clare's – and later, the classics: *The Mill on the Floss, Silas Marner, Jane Eyre, Wuthering Heights*. So when I walked down Broad Street or High Street as an undergraduate at Oxford, amid those medieval stones with their spires, dreaming, it felt strangely familiar. I thought, with some embarrassment, of the Australians, New Zealanders, and Anglo-Indians who still call England home. For Oxford felt like the landscape of my imagination, of literature. Architecture, majestic, yet restrained and elegant. Air breathing history. Hopkins' lines swelled in memory – *Ah! this air I gather and I release/He lived on; these weeds and waters, these walls are what/He haunted who of all men most sways my spirits to peace*, he wrote of the medieval theologian, Duns Scotus. How esoteric! The people who I remembered, with a frisson of pleasure, had lived at the Oxford colleges through which I wandered, studied in the Bodleian, matriculated under the gargoyles of the Sheldonian were Gerard Manley Hopkins himself, and Matthew Arnold who first conjured the magic of Oxford for me: *And that sweet city with her dreaming spires, she needs not June for beauty's heightening*. That's where I would have chosen to live – England where I spent three exuberant years, and, later, three dreamy, beauty-soaked vacations. I feel more of an affinity with it than with my India, the elbowy crowds, the noise and tumult, "the huddled masses." Coleridge on a Scotsman: "He was geographically slandered by the place of his birth."

What is home? Familiar earth? Where you grew up? Where people speak your native language? Where those you love live? And a place where you can relax? I no longer, of course, consider my parents' house, home. It's now my mother's domain. I feel out of my element in her home; when I am there, so does she. India no longer feels like home. My parents have moved from Jamshedpur where I grew up to Bangalore, a retiree hub, India's "garden city," and its Silicon Valley. Bangalore is Babel: Telegu, Tamil, Kannada, Konkani, English, Hindi – and my Hindi, once fluent, after seventeen years in England and America, is fluttering away, evanescent as languages not used. When I travel overseas, I have the sense of coming home when I reach the United States. When I travel alone, I feel I am at home when my husband and daughters meet me at the airport. And then, the rapture, the sheer sensuous pleasure, the sense of relaxation of inhabiting, once more, 104 Richard's Patent, Williamsburg, Virginia, the home and garden I have worked – as leisure and money show their fleeting faces – on making beautiful, the garden singing and bright with birds at the feeders, fluttering in season with swallowtail butterflies around our butterfly puddles and sweet flowers.

I suppose the spirit has its deepest roots in the place it returns to in dreams. My dreams are set in two locales: the home I grew up in in Jamshedpur, India – spacious, sixteen rooms, airy, whitewashed, high-ceilinged, with a huge garden, dense with fruit trees, flowers, and vegetables; and my boarding school, St. Mary's Convent, in Nainital in the Himalayas. My spirit was formed there, rather than in Jamshedpur, which was not beautiful, though it had pretty parks, with lakes and islands, rose gardens, and flood-lit rainbowed fountains. But in Nainital, I became myself, evolved – long quiet hours, much time to read and dream in that valley above the limpid Naini lake, surrounded by towering mountains. The Himalayas have imprinted their topography on my soul. Ever since school, I feel restless for the green sweep of mountains and the music of streams.

Their belief in things invisible, and in a way without guaranteed tangible rewards, made the great men of faith exiles, says a New Testament writer – "aliens and strangers on earth." Like them, though not with a purposive displacement, I've always felt slightly alien, transplanted, "a minority," a Catholic in Hindu India; an ethnic South Indian growing up in the north; and then, in a further displacement, my boarding school was in the extreme north of India, in the foothills of the Himalayas. Strangely, I never felt at home in the North Indian town I grew up in, Jamshedpur in Bihar. My parents were not natives. My mother grew up in Bombay; the family of my father, the son of the first Indian Civil Surgeon in the Empire, was continually transferred all over the South. He moved to Jamshedpur after eight years studying and working in England. My parents looked down on the life around them: Bihari *Buddus*, idiots, they called the locals in a common alliterative insult (often applying the slur to me, for I was born in Bihar!) They lived in a parallel universe, keeping meticulous notes on the four to five Western movies they watched each week in the three private clubs they belonged to, and of every book they read, English language or in translation, Gide, Camus, Woolf, Huxley, Orwell.

Like them, I grew up with a faint sense of unlikeness, displacement, so much so that to be an amphibian now feels swimming in a native element, half in water, half in the starry air, a stranger in both worlds, never quite belonging anywhere. I read different stuff, and more, often dreaming the day away, my soul immersed in a book, as if I were drifting in a boat in a lazy river, a sense I've not often had after abruptly quitting my Ph.D program for marriage and its enforced extroversion. My mother collected fading cloth-bound books for me from well-educated old friends and extended family members who no longer read. I read the classics, again and again, gravitating to the piles of them in the house, appealing to an aimless moment, ignorant yet of Matthew Arnold's dictum that life is too short to read anything but the best that has been said and thought (a wise statement, though it can paralyze the joyous exploration of reading: *perhaps something better has been written*). I soon had more books in my room than in the children's bookcase of the local library, most of which I'd read – except those that seemed meant for boys: adventures around the world; up in the air; under the sea; ships, pirates, coral islands – nah! I invited classmates on pilgrimages to my room to see my shrine of books on hand-built shelves, floor to ceiling, which I read again and again, books in a language not spoken around me in the marketplace, or street, or by the three servants in the house – *Lamb's Tales from Shakespeare*, Norse mythology, Greek mythology, poetry... "You are a square peg in a round hole," my father shook his head.

I do not hear ancestral voices when I write the language I love – the native language of England imposed on India by conquest. Playing with its plasticity gives a shape and excitement to my days. I revel in its words and their antique history as in an heirloom. I want my daughters, Zoe and Irene, to savor its beauty and sensuous pleasure – then feel a dissonance. Its history is barely allied with those who share my blood; it did not evolve on my native soil; . I speak it because of a legacy of conquest and bitterness. "The Conquistadors took our gold, but they left us their gold: they left us our words," Carlos Fuentes shrugs. I watched Hermione Lee of the B.B.C. interview R.K. Narayan who looked like a traditional Indian patriarch. "Why do you write in English?" Lee asked, gently. "Because it is the language I know best," he said, equally simply. "If I knew any language better, I would write in it."

And, in a double displacement, I believe in a religion forced, nearly 350 years ago, on my ancestors in Mangalore, though I am no longer a Roman Catholic but a mere Christian. All the picturesque trappings of Catholicism have sloughed away. Transubstantiation, saints, purgatory, rosaries, novenas: they no longer figure in my spiritual life. But I still believe in the gorgeous proposition that God entered human history in that zero year. Christ, his teachings: that's the zigzag that helps me make sense of the jigsaw of life, and find a tranquil joy in it. Oh, lots of things bring me pleasure – my children, my writing, my garden, literature, paintings, film, nature, family life, friendships, travel, thinking – but following Christ unites the disparate chords into a rich and abounding symphony that swirls in the sadness that accompanies joy as moonlight follows the brightest day.

In considering my life a story being written by God, I apprehend, amid the randomness and anguish, a plot. I find in faith what Arnold found in love: consolation amid chaos, life's truest meaning. *Ah, love, let us be true/ To one another! for the world,/ which seems/ To lie before us like a land of dreams,/ So various, so beautiful, so new,/ Hath really neither joy, nor love, nor light,/ Nor certitude, nor peace, nor help for pain*, Arnold cried. I cry, "Ah, love, let us believe, for in itself this world *hath really neither joy, nor love, nor light,/ Nor certitude, nor peace, nor help for pain...*"

I no longer base my identity on my race, or education, or profession: a writer. I attempt to shed my old identity to graft myself into, and orient myself by the majestic, luminous figure of Christ "the radiance of God's glory," "in whom all things hang together." I now define myself by my faith :I am a mere Christian. In the quiet steady light of Christ, I attempt to make sense the sadness of life ("the vale of soul-making," Keats describes it) I glimpse in the destitute on the streets of Bangalore, and in the strained eyes of faculty at a college garden party in Williamsburg – what Virgil called "the tears of things."

I settled down, eight years ago, in Williamsburg, Virginia, where I have no roots except – ironically, paradoxically – actual physical roots, for this is where I live. If I were a woman of vast independent income, or an athlete, ballet dancer, ex-dictator, or high-profile victim of an ex-dictator that would enable me to take refuge anywhere I chose, I would have chosen Oxford, England – *Towery city and branchy between towers; Cuckoo-echoing, bell-swarmed, lark-charmed, rook-racked, river-rounded* – where I spent three of the most formative, and certainly exhilarated years of my life. Two glorious worlds – Art and nature – within an easy bike ride. Tidewater Virginia does not lack natural beauty, but "high art" entails a long drive.

I feel no affinity with the slave-owning colonists who settled here in Williamsburg – land hunters, tobacco farmers, saturating the soil with blood, tears, sweat and greed, aspiring to transcend their status and become landed gentry. Tobacco planters! What have I in common with them? I inwardly growl. If I had to choose a place to live in America, it might be one of those villages outside Boston with literary associations, Concord or Amherst. I love the heady, pure wintry air of the literature of nineteenth century New England – Emerson, Thoreau, Hawthorne, Melville, Dickinson... And I share religious roots and a sensibility with New England Puritans such as Jonathan Edwards, their fervid faith, their passionate absolutist souls, the poetic intensity with which they saw a black and white universe charged with divine meanings, *liber mundi*, God's book of the world, through which He revealed himself in metaphors, spiders suggesting divine allegories.

I did not get to choose; life chose for me. Lacking "five hundred pounds a year," I could not make my home anywhere I wished, and I didn't want to work a job – which gives you mobility (assuming you can get one). My husband sent off applications in the scattershot fashion that computers abet. And then because we were young – and when you are young, you are sanguine, for the future stretches infinitely in front of you, and your nerves are as elastic as your body; and the fellowship to Stanford and Cornell Roy had after he graduated from Johns Hopkins was winding down – he accepted the first job he was offered: Assistant Professor of Mathematics at the College of William and Mary, Williamsburg, Virginia. Where was that? My fingers traced a map. Oh well, we could move.

Except that in Williamsburg, willy-nilly, roots started their secret insistent work. "Roots, roots of remembered greenery, traverse long distances by surmounting some obstacles, penetrating others, and insinuating themselves into narrow cracks," Nabokov muses. My psychic and emotional roots surmounted some obstacles, penetrated others, and insinuated themselves into narrow cracks. I now feel, more or less, at home – though it's not the place I have chosen, but the place I have accepted.

Friends came, more slowly than I wished, but eventually, after wrenching growth in solitude. I can now find my friends' houses without getting lost, a feat for me who invariably got lost, when I left my house in Minneapolis (another place in which I could have joyfully settled) driving the wrong way up a one-way street, exiting a highway at the last moment, cutting recklessly in front of trucks, the upturned wriggling fingers – and it was the wrong exit! I can now get to the library without horns or fingers. Life is slow here, road rage rare. And, gradually, we realized that we had begun to put down roots. We are at home. We do not plan to leave the orchard we have planted, the herb garden, the flower beds, the pond we've dug in the backyard which reflects the woods around it, and soothes the eyes and soul, extending an almost irresistible invitation to sit and be still. I have another project. If you cannot make your home in Eden – then in a kind of judo, literally "the gentle way," turning adversity to your advantage – make your home Eden. Once you cease rebelling against the constrictions of your life, you can use them to grow as an espaliered fruit tree uses walls. There's a strength in accepting defeat. *That's that.* Now let's see if we can rebound from it. I think of the Greek monster, Antaeus. Pushed to the earth, his mother, he derived strength from that low place, and rose stronger than before.

I felt alien in Williamsburg for a long time. I'd pray, "Oh Lord, let me bloom where I am planted," and then cry, for I couldn't imagine blooming in this little town with little in the way of a literary community, theater, art. After five years in Williamsburg, I met again a well-known essayist I had studied with in Minneapolis, a more literary city. He read my work and said, "What's happened to you? Your sentences have changed. You've become a writer." In the apparently barren years, without the distraction that so easily distracts, I began to learn, belatedly, to focus. Winter – the lack of abundant sun and water – sends roots down, deep into the soil, seeking nourishment. Similarly, creativity can bloom in winter if you explore the present and its tangles; and the deep past, and taste the pleasures of thinking. Rilke counsels – *Even if you found yourself in some prison, whose walls let in none of the world's sounds – wouldn't you still have your childhood, that jewel beyond all price, that treasure house of memories? Turn your attention to it. Try to raise up the sunken feeling of this enormous past; your personality will grow stronger, your solitude will expand and become a place where you can live in the twilight, where the noise of other people passes by, far in the distance.*

I have begun to relish living in a place for a long time, being rooted and grounded in it, making and leaving my mark on the landscape, greeting each season with bulbs I have planted. I love watching the natural year wheel from the picture window at which I write – the kuk-kuk-kuk of the pileated woodpecker resounding through the woods, tiger swallowtails fluttering in their mating dance, bluebirds on the purple spray of eastern redbud each spring; hummingbirds amid the trumpet vine in the summer; red-bellied woodpeckers alighting on the flaming sweetgum in the fall; the trees alive with migrant birds in the winter. Rooted, you can begin to form long friendships. And small towns offer a sense of community, even if it's a pseudo-sense. Still, even in Williamsburg,

Virginia, dizzily growing, familiar groves cut down by the day for frivolous upscale stores, and gated communities of mansions for retirees, I – almost every time I leave my house to go to the library, gym, store, or to walk in that pleasing fake antique, Colonial Williamsburg – see people I know (by name, face, or intimate detail) through my writing; the college my husband, and, occasionally, I teach at; church, children, the neighborhood; and we feel nebulous goodwill as we meet.

Being settled is a relief. For ten years, my home address metamorphosed: Madras, India; Oxford, England; Columbus, Ohio; Binghamton, New York; Ithaca, New York; Palo Alto, California; Minneapolis, Minnesota, and then, Williamsburg, Virginia. Before our sixth wedding anniversary – those gypsy years of post-doctoral research and early career! – my husband and I made seven homes, in four states. The sound of the list wearies me, all those moves and UPS boxes and change of address forms. Now I wish for us, and for our daughters, what Yeats wished for his daughter,

"Oh, may she live like some green laurel,
Rooted in one dear perpetual place."

Through luck, or grace unsought, I have quite possibly found this place, a half acre of dear land, a tapestry deep, rich, and green, I gaze at through the large windows facing the woods in the backyard,. I enjoy returning to my home after my eccentric late night rambles to put recalcitrant babies to sleep. It shines like a sanctuary in the woods, warm and welcoming, or conversely, makes me think of a white, airy cabin of a ship, glowing bright on the seas.

The boundary lines have fallen for me in pleasant places, as the Psalmist says. After I bought a house and planted an orchard around it, in a symbolic gesture of putting down roots, I feel quieter, settled, as if my life has put down roots in my house and garden. Both ground me, sometimes literally. I've discovered, after years of believing the fallacy of the bohemian, impulse-driven artist – what I now think of as the wasted years of indiscipline, reading till three or four a.m., waking up at noon or one – the fertility of an orderly, peaceful life, like nature, lovely, and on schedule. The crawling of woolly bears; the migration of monarchs and snow geese; snowflakes and spring blossoms; how predictable – but how shiveringly lovely. "It is good to be regular and orderly in your life, so that you may be violent and original in your work," wrote Flaubert, artist of artists. Art from the fecund soil of a disciplined life – keeping my house beautiful and orderly, tending my garden, nurturing children. Such imperatives can function as scaffolding for the artist, roots anchoring the enormous sycamore. They stave off depression and torpor.

The house is ballast, an anchor. After the intensity of writing in which you lose track of everyone and everything around you as you wrestle to the page words and their meanings, you return to the ground base of your home, puttering, cleaning, organizing, and this stabilizing manual work serves as the fixed pole of the compass, a Penelope from which your art journeys, to which it returns. A house, clean, few things in it, everything beautiful and in its place, radiates quietness, an invitation to relax, be still, work, love, be. The tranquil home is the wrist from which the peregrine imagination can soar to return with its prize; the axis from which productivity flows, contentment, and the making and enjoying of beauty.

In addition to the traditional monastic vows of poverty, chastity, and obedience, Benedictine monks made a commitment to "stability," to stay in their chosen monastery, on their elected spot of earth, until death. What a sane idea! When we bought our house, we planted dozens of hostas, hundreds of bulbs and perennials, and espaliered pear trees along the walls, putting down roots with every intention of staying put. Barring biological accidents: more children, paralysis... I cannot conceive why I would want something bigger. Or smaller. It's probably easier for the spirit to stretch its wings in large airy spaces.

The roots of a mighty oak delve into the soil. The deeper they dive, the higher they can soar. What does the oak sacrifice for the height to which it wanders? Mobility. Traveling out of Concord. I have traded the buzz of intellectual, cultural, and aesthetic stimulation in headier places, Oxford, Cambridge, Minneapolis, Boston to live quietly, acquainting myself with the history, natural history, and joys of the land I've found myself in, and to enjoy the settled pleasures of rootedness. It's a form of scholarship, staying put, "traveling a good deal in Concord," in Thoreau's phrase, being a specialist rather than a generalist. For to put down roots – to eliminate the distraction and turbulence of mobility – permits one to grow and flower; to concentrate on yielding creative and spiritual fruit.

A blessing granted to the righteous in the Old Testament was to be rooted "like a tree planted by streams of water, which yields its fruit in season, and whose leaf does not wither" whereas the unrighteous were like chaff that the wind blows away. To be rootless was deemed a curse in that agrarian society. Satan, in *Job*, was restless, "roaming through the earth and going back and forth in it." The curse on Cain: "To be a restless wanderer on the earth."

Rootlessness is like a curse in modern America where people move every three to four years. The consequent uprooting and disorientation, the lack of long, deep friendships, and the loneliness, all precipitate the epidemic of depression psychologists describe. According to psychiatrist Antonio Wood, the mobility of families, coupled with the breakdown of the nuclear family, is predisposing the entire culture to depression. "The most important factor in the growing incidence of depression is social isolation," Wood suggests. "We're really social animals. If we are taken out of the pack, we die."

To be rootless, to have no home except in my writing that travels with me wherever I go, now seems as sad to me as the curse of legend on the Wandering Jew: to roam the world until Christ's second coming. No, I would like, also, to be rooted in the familiar: in a beloved garden, and a beloved house, lived in, improved, made more beautiful through the years, that – like a fossil, or amber encasing dragonflies – will be a silent record of my life in it.

Transplantation is never an experiment without peril. Transplants need to be performed in a beneficent season, tended carefully, given compost and extra water. Sometimes for a few weeks or months, the tree appears to thrive, or at least survive, and then, inexplicably, the leaves yellow; the trunk browns; you scratch the bark, and nowhere does it show green, and you know it's lost, like those survivors of the unthinkable, living testaments to the resiliency of the human spirit, who decades later, disappointing their mythologizers, kill themselves when everything is apparently at its best, a straw igniting old fires, until without warning, the spirit and nervous system snap.

Not all trees survive transplantation, or succeed in putting down roots in alien soil to thrive. Immigration – a rude and global transplantation – is a stressor not to be undertaken lightly. For there is no telling which transplants will take.

When I study the faces of immigrants, the lostness, the strain of the attempt to sing an old song in an alien land, I wonder if it was worth it. If immigration opens up a way to taste life in its fullness, perhaps it can be justified. For people whose deepest satisfaction is in their work, immigration works out for good, I guess, if it offers a larger, more fulfilling arena for their lifework. It's a great trade-in. You trade in your roots – landscape, possessions, family, friends, connections, social standing, all things familiar that made up your world – to heed the siren summons to adventure in fresh woods and pastures new. In a sense, you change your very identity. In India, from my features, my coloring, my clothes, my accent, people could, with uncanny accuracy, surmise much of my identity, and place me as I could place them: could often tell that I was a Catholic, educated, upper-middle class, a Mangalorean or a Goan, communities that were converted to Catholicism in the mid-sixteenth century by the Portuguese, and intermarried with the colonizers. As an immigrant, you lose your old identity. People now suspect me of being from Nicaragua, Granada, Cuba, Libya, Lebanon, Iraq, Aghanistan, whichever country America is currently shaking its mighty finger at.

What a mind-boggling uprooting immigration is! Yet even as a teenager, I itched to leave India and strike out for the West. It seemed a larger, freer world, the world of the literature I loved. I wanted to live in England, but my visa forbade work, so to America I drifted. England still seems green and pleasant in contrast to America, a land that works, often soulless in its efficiency, rushed, rushing to the bitter end. To find poetry, mystery, and magic in America, I think one must become a naturalist. That's where I have found romance and delight – in thermal pools like morning glories in Yellowstone; in shaggy herds of bison shambling across the road in the Badlands; in the intertidal pools of the Fitzgerald Marine Reserve and the seal colonies of the Ano Nuevo State Reserve in the Bay Area; in Arcadia, Yellowstone, Yosemite, Mount Rainier, the Grand Tetons, and Shenandoah. The ancient universe of nature, pristine, magical.

Was immigration worth it for me? Yes. I felt cabined, cribbed, confined in India. My family's litany was: "What will people think?" "What will people say?" I wanted to be free of that conformist society and its expectations. I wanted to gulp experience, to explore the world like Larry of *The Razor's Edge*, a teenage hero. I enjoyed escaping from my family – a great advantage of immigration. I wrenched up my roots for the freedom of anonymity; the latitude offered by the variety of ways to behave and be; for privacy and the quiet to work; and for the facets of Western culture that exhilarate me – art galleries, ballet, film, theater, and, of course, contemporary literature. I am not sorry I have transplanted myself.

Though the perspective with which I think and feel and view the world was formed in India, and when I sit down to write – the immigrant irony! – I draw on its mountains, rivers, and winds. For much that I absorbed as mother's milk, embers that still glow in my imagination, is, of course, from India – the poetry of Tagore; the great epic, the *Ramayana*, with the lonely scrupulous figure of Ram, who set aside his blameless wife Sita, after she was abducted by the demon king, Ravana, even though she had not been ravished – an early exemplar of the morality of a society where appearance and reputation count for everything. And the *Mahabharata* with its beautiful heroine, Draupadi, common wife of the five Pandava brothers, who gambled her away to their cousins, the Kauravas; when the victors attempt to publicly strip her, Draupadi's saree magically stretches even as it was unraveled. Avenging her, the hero Arjuna, in a panic attack before the battle of Kurukshetra, lyrically agonizes in the *Bhagvad Gita* on the stern requirements of duty which required him to kill the kinsman amassed against him. And then, the story of history – Asoka, converted to Buddhism, planting trees along the famous Grand Trunk Road; the Muslim "Slave Dynasty," slave succeeding slave as King; the fascinating, psychologically complex Mughal Emperors, inventing religions, erecting perennially lovely buildings, the Red Fort, the Moti Masjid, and the elegant Taj Mahal, cool marble inlaid, in ornate pietra dura, with precious stones, in which once as a child, escaping from a guided tour, I got lost. And I think of the Indian freedom movement with fascination, a triumph of character, conviction, and morality over might – or so it appears.

Perhaps because I have mostly been a house mouse, after seventeen years the West retains an aura of strangeness. And I would not trade this shimmering sense of "something rich and strange" to be the bored child of privilege. Cycling on the towpaths by the Isis; walking Oxford streets at night among the Gothic spires, yearning skywards; sauntering dreamily on Addison's Walk by the Cherwell, that trembled with daffodils: things that might seem a birthright to one more privileged, gave me the sense of living in a beneficent dream. I needed to leave India for the experiences most branded on my memory – pattering water in Bernini's fountain at the Spanish Steps, near the room in which Keats died, musing, *All your better deeds shall lie in water writ*; lapping waves near the island graveyard of San Michele, in Venice; strolling beside the canal in Kyoto, bright with cherry blossoms; Botticelli in the Uffizi.

Given hindsight, would I leave India again? Without a doubt, sooner than I did before. I was chafing to escape my conventional, constrained community in which apparently innocuous words and actions fertilized gossip. Though, of course, there is a cost, a psychic cost. You ponder racism, ugly word; wonder if you are being treated differently because of your honeyed skin. Are the slow waiters inefficient, lazy – or racist? People might assume that you do not know how the system works (and you might not) so you are never sure if you are as well-served as one with whiter skin. Strangers screw their faces in anticipation as you open your mouth. Annoyingly, your accent is not always understood. Your Otherness: a source of stress, and gaffes, for yourself and others.

But returning will be no easier. As a bear tamed by humans cannot survive in the wild, moving back to India would be a culture shock of its own. The skills of swiftly grabbing an empty seat, of jumping lines have faded away. You would wait to be served, futilely, interminably, instead of hollering in the crowd thronging around the counter. How impotent this politeness in a society where only losers stand and wait.

Now, I *really* feel displaced. I suppose immigration is a way of finding solitude, the solitude of floating away from the anchoring past. You become an alien and a stranger on the earth, like those ancient men and women of faith. In fact, the Biblical writers observe that we are all exiles and strangers on earth where we have no lasting city, restless until we find our rest and completion in the vast sea of God: the deep peace at the heart of the hurricane, the only lasting solace and anchor for our jumpy spirits; our true home, where alone we belong.

And, I must say, exile is good for a writer. Even as her wondering, innocent eyes survey her new land starkly, freshly, all her journeying helps her see her old land clearly, as if for the first time. Its very contrast with the present, so efficient, so mechanized, so fast, gives memories of the past the sharpness of an etching. Its essence is so different that biting into a similarity, a madeleine say, sparks a magic lantern show of remembrance. Like the image that emerges as you trace over metal, the past surfaces in all its sensuousness. In the quiet of the present exile, it floats, a remote mountain castle, brightly silhouetted against the sky.

7 | The First Thing in the Morning

Exercise first thing in the morning, my fitness instructor says. The discipline will spill over to the rest of the day. It jumpstarts your metabolism, so that you burn more calories, whether you read or cook or nap. And if you wake early enough, you can walk on the golf course.

Pray first thing in the morning, the radio preacher thunders. Jesus rose before the dawn to pray to his heavenly father. Pray before phone-calls and mail and frustrations jangle your spirit; pray while your mind is clear and tranquil, and you can hear what the Lord God has to say. The plug of prayer connects you to the power you need for the day.

Write first in the morning, my professor advises. The only way to learn to write is by writing. And that way you're sure you've done it. Your unconscious is closer to its dream state early in the morning. It can fly. He quotes Goethe: "Write at dawn, skim the cream of the day, then you can study crystals, intrigue at court, and make love to your kitchen maid." Trollope rose at 5:30 a.m. to write; he wrote seventy books. Hemingway rose at six, wrote till midday, and then had fun.

But read before you write, the teacher adds. Books come from other books. The rhythms of your mentor will throb in your veins; they will pulse through your own writing.

Study your dreams which offer you the wisdom of the unconscious, my therapist suggests. Your dream of arriving late to a party you're hosting, arriving after the glutted guests couldn't care less about you, is an admonition that you are working too hard. You are missing the party of your life. Record your dreams first thing in the morning. Delay ten minutes and you forget the dream; its details blur.

Do difficult things first thing in the morning, I note at the brown-bag lecture, "Organize Yourself." The longer you delay, the tireder you grow, the harder seems the task. "Procrastination makes easy things difficult, and difficult things impossible."

The alarm shrills at five a.m. The dog wants to go out. The coffee must be brewed. I must brush my teeth and wash my face and comb my hair. I must be quiet, or I will wake the baby.

Voices sound around me, mentors and tormentors. Drink lemon and honey the first thing in the morning; it purifies the blood. Pray, exercise, read, write, record your dreams – the first thing in the morning. The world comes at me. I duck under the comforter.

I wake, much later, to the baby's first cry. I write this the last thing at night.

8 | Writing and Prayer

Writing and Prayer. We read about them, write about them, talk about them, agonize about them, resolve to do them, wish we'd done them, more than we actually do them. In this they resemble other pursuits that people overestimate the intensity, frequency, and duration of – reading, and sex.

Both writing and prayer are archaic, anachronistic, against the grain of modern life, solitary and often heartbreaking, embarked on without the certainty of fruit. Both demand an expenditure, an apparent waste of time, that's like a waste of self. Bill Gates in *Time* magazine: "In terms of allocation of time resources, religion is not very efficient. There's a lot more I could be doing on Sunday morning." Of course, of course. Making art is not the most efficient use of time either when it comes to tangible economic rewards. It's working in the darkness with no guarantees of success, publication, or "fame, money, and the love of beautiful people." Now or ever. It's working with blind faith, stubborn hope, dumb love.

The tiny stunted wings of the flightless cormorant of the Galapagos are useless for flying. Yet with hazy, ancestral memories of flight, it spends much of its time standing on rocks near the shore spreading its vestigial wings out to dry in the sun, just as flying cormorants do. Flapping wings with a sense of futility, a foreboding of failure. That's how we feel on the brink of something difficult, but exhilarating like writing or prayer. But if the wind suddenly lifted the bird and it sailed through the skies, effortlessly, beautifully – well, that's like flight into the realm where the right words in the right order surprise like a free gift; ideas cascade, inevitable as a cataract; and each sentence sings; or in prayer when "so great a sweetness flows in the breast that we must laugh and we must sing, we are blest by everything, everything we look upon is blest."

In both prayer and writing, these blessed states are partly a free gift, and partly earned: we travail to forge the metal which lightning may strike. Both take a quiet life, hard work, and sacrifice. Henry James captures the pain: "If one would do the best he can with his pen, there is one word he must inscribe on his banner, and that word is *solitude*." Though there have, of course, been gregarious writers – I think of Trollope who treasured the social success, the club life, and the friends his writing brought him – and though friendships bring insight, knowledge, self-knowledge, and growth, my own experience echoes T.S. Eliot in "Ash Wednesday," "Where shall the word be found, where will the word/ Resound? Not here, there is not enough silence." Conversations echo in my head, a dissonance drowning out my own thoughts. Too much extroversion robs me of the inner quiet necessary to view my life sanely, leave alone to revise it. In fact, my writing and my thinking are inversely proportional to my social life.

"Be still and know that I am God," echoes an Old Testament imperative. In the Book of Kings, the Lord appeared to the prophet Elijah, not in "the great and powerful wind that tore the mountains apart and shattered the rocks," not in the earthquake, not in the fire, but in "a gentle whisper." A whisper, easily drowned in the tumult of an overambitious schedule. The Quaker writer, Richard Foster, extols the otium sanctum, "holy leisure," of the Church Fathers. "If we expect to succeed in the contemplative arts, we must pursue "holy leisure" with a determination that is ruthless to our date books," he says.

Holy Leisure. It is indeed the best soil for writing or prayer: a considered, underscheduled and life with fallow hours, and pruned activities, commitments, friends. It's important especially for women, trained to be "nice," to perfect the difficult art of saying No, resisting the blandishments to busyness, "giving back to the community," taking your turn, doing your fair share. Not to do as much as – possibly – you can, but to live with "the broad margin to life," Thoreau praises, thus making space for the new idea, the transforming insight. When I look at Vermeer's paintings, the girl pausing in the midst of quiet work to gaze out of the window and muse, I think: That is how I want to live my life, softly, meditatively, reverently. Coming to the quietness has a cost, of course, the cost of the loneliness that wrenches you when the quietness you have courted seems more than you can bear. Precious, costly, and priceless, that holy loneliness, carved out and set apart from the dead wood of lunches, dinner parties, and talk, talk, talk.

We enter the realm of paradoxes. Though we need solitude to pray, prayer returns to the engagement of love. The refrain of "The Rime of the Ancient Mariner" long embroidered into samplers declares, "He prayeth well who loveth well/ Both man and bird and beast./ He prayeth best who loveth best/ All things both great and small." John, Jesus' beloved friend, gives us two yardsticks to gauge our spirituality – growing love for God, growing love for the people in our lives. Real prayer does not so much change God's mind as it changes us, slowly, almost imperceptibly. And in the quietness of prayer, we learn the arts of kindness. Thomas Merton in *New Seeds of Contemplation*: "It is in deep solitude that I find the gentleness with which I can truly love my brothers. The more solitary I am, the more affection I have for them. It is pure affection and filled with reverence for the solitude of others. Solitude and silence teach me to love my brothers for what they are, not for what they say."

And though there have been splendid lyric poets like Emily Dickinson who were essentially recluses, drawing inspiration from the certain slant of light on winter afternoons, much of the inexhaustible art like *Hamlet, Lear, Madame Bovary, Middlemarch*, or *Wuthering Heights* that shares its wisdom and beauty with you afresh on each encounter, springs from the empathy from which Flaubert declares, "Madame Bovary, c'est moi." That's interesting considering a writer's actual work, faced with the blank page, is quiet to the point of sensory deprivation. Just as a foreigner sees the quirks and oddities of a country more clearly than the native, the person who deliberately seeks solitude gains clear-sightedness. I like that line of Yeats, "And eyes by solitary thought made aquiline."

Whether one seeks to be an artist or a contemplative, discipline, mundane word, must channel the streams of sweetness that surprise, whether "inspiration," or the rapturous insights of contemplation. We've heard the metaphor: inspiration, like lightning, strikes where it wills, whom it wills. But if anything lasting, anything lovely, is to remain after its sudden blazing descent, there is no substitute for the long hours of learning a craft. This apprenticeship teaches us to tame a torrent of ideas in sinuous, sinewy sentences, in the essay's narrow room. (And, as with any craft, and this is one of life's unfairnesses, there are the naturals who absorb the tricks of the trade rapidly, as if by osmosis, and others, of whom I am one, who learn them slowly, arduously).

In fact, inspiration is a way of seeing, a loving perception of the mystery, the magic, the tiny miracles in daily life that we can train ourselves to acquire. It takes slowing down. Consider the subjects that the house-bound Emily Dickinson made poetry of – the fly, the bird, the worm, the snake. Traveling through the hours lightly, looking, thinking, helps our eyes cultivate the retina of wonder, the ability to "see a world in a grain of sand, and a heaven in a wild flower, hold infinity in the palm of your hand, and eternity in an hour."

Writing a literary book feels like tunneling through the Himalayas with a spade. You work in the darkness with no surety that you'll ever succeed, just wild hope. You just do it, and do it, and do it, and you probably do it best when you do it without hope of reward – for its own sake. In "Writing in the Cold," his brilliant essay on the writing life, the editor Ted Solotaroff suggests that "the turning point in many people's writing lives was when the intrinsic interest of what they were doing began to take over, and generate a sense of necessity." The intrinsic interest rather than ambition, or restlessness for reward: money, praise, "the buzz."

There's always the intermittent temptation to abandon being a writer, or being a Christian. I have, at moments of crushing discouragement, contemplated giving up writing altogether. But then I know I cannot. There will always be empty hours. I cannot imagine living without a passion to fill them, and nothing for me is more interesting. And so I continue like Macbeth after the first murder that necessitated sequential crimes: "I am steeped in blood so far, that returning were as tedious as going o'er." So I work dumbly, doggedly, like a ox plodding in circles, treading grain. To modify Eliot's stricture in "The Four Quartets," I work and "wait without hope/ For hope would be hope for the wrong thing; work and wait without love/ For love would be love of the wrong thing; there is yet faith/ But the faith and the hope and the love are all in the waiting./ For us there is only the trying. The rest is not our business," Eliot concludes.

Writing early drafts feels like groping in the darkness – like reaching for God who is somewhere in the shadows, loving and good, powerful and wise. And amid the griefs of life – a precious friendship dissolves amid gossip and misunderstandings, the book manuscript I've worked on for five years is not viable, when I feel pierced by "the arrow that flies by night," inexplicable malice, envy, betrayal, the human depravity scripture details – I grope for him, trying to see the meaning, the final draft, when all around me is a mess of manuscript, haphazard, crossed-out, added-to. And I try to revise myself and my life beyond the first draft, believing that with the help of the sovereign wise artificer, this manuscript of aspirations will eventually become the finished, completed, perfect book.

While practicing both arts, you yearn for acceleration. You get fed up of this trying and failing; you want to write well; you want to master your craft. You want to savor the joy, and the peace that passeth understanding that lured you onwards. But spiritual growth is slow and gradual. The good man in the Psalms is compared to "a tree planted by streams of water, which yields its fruit *in due season*." Evolving as an artist is a similarly organic process. The natural can master her craft more rapidly by a ferocity of hours and will, diligence and discipline, but wisdom comes in its own time. That's why it's hard to think of a writer who has been a child prodigy, a Mozart.

Yet, though nothing but time can turn a sapling into the largest of trees, so that the birds of the air come and perch on its branches, there are organic fertilizers for one's tender spiritual or artistic life, that will help it grow stronger, lovelier, and, yes, faster. Reading widely and deeply, the old masters as well as new ones; writing carefully and continually for writing is an art one learns by doing; seeking out smart criticism to show you your blind spots; creating time and space to work quietly – these help a writer develop. A fierce yearning – "God-hunger" – launches spiritual growth. "You shall seek me, and you shall find me when you seek me with all your heart." Jeremiah's words were engraved on a plaque in our dormitory when I was a novice with Mother Teresa at Calcutta. Yearning and seeking – but also making time to meditate on Scripture, discipline in obeying its wisdom. Though spiritual maturity will come in its own time, these practices might hasten that day.

And in both arts, like a shadow behind the bright yearning for perfection, is the inevitability of failure. The Apostle Paul laments this in a poignant, brilliant passage: *"I do not understand what I do. For I have the desire to do what is good, but I cannot carry it out. For what I do is not the good I want to do; no, the evil I do not want to do – this I keep on doing.*

So I find this law at work: When I want to do good, evil is right there with me. For in my inner being, I delight in God's law; but I see another law at work in the members of my body, waging war against the law of my mind and making me a prisoner of the law of sin. What a wretched man I am!

Failure – or, theologically, sin – is the antiphon to our yearning for goodness; to be loving; to be, in the Biblical word, righteous. But through it all, through the valley of failure, emerges a faint, pointillist likeness to Christ. You are changed as you seek to imitate Christ, and more, to be merged with him, to be blood brothers in the ancient sense, and have his sweet life flow through you as sap through a vine, in his metaphor.

When I write, I desire beauty in my inmost being. I want my sentences to be as iridescent as Nabokov's, as grave and freighted and precise as Alice Munro's, as haunting as Keats' or Hopkins' or Sylvia Plath's. I want to create essays as lovely as a bough quivering with spring blossoms or glistening with icicles. I do not see this in my drafts. Wretched woman that I am, what will rescue me from this imperfect work? Time might, and hard work might, and reading constantly and critically might.

Or perhaps nothing will. I may never be Nabokov or Rushdie, my favorite prose stylists. John Gardner claims that more people fail at becoming successful businessmen than at becoming writers. If so, I must know many of the unsuccessful, for I know many who write hard, and read hard, and long hard for success, but whom success eludes, who have very minor careers at best. Solotaroff, less encouragingly, looks at the young writers full of bright promise that he published in the "New American Review," and estimates that one-quarter go on to have reasonably successful careers; one-quarter have marginal ones in the alternative literary community of the little magazines and small presses; and one half simply disappear.

What separates the writer who emerges from the one who disappears? These help budding talent flower – the time and quiet to write, the stimulation and encouragement of the literary community, the support of family, adequate money and privacy: "500 pounds a year and a room of one's own" – a concatenation of happy circumstances. When I read biographies of writers, I am struck by how their development as artists was aided by "luck" – a crucial nurturing friendship with a mentor or a fellow writer in their formative years, the zigzags of life leading to the books, paintings, cities, teachers, friends they needed to blossom. As the old weary book of Ecclesiastes observes, "The race is not to the swiftest, nor does food come to the wise, or wealth to the brilliant, or favor to the learned, but time and chance happen to them all." On the other hand, luck does tend to happen to gifted people who work hard. And good writing is the best connection, the best "in" to the loop.

And then there's "talent," arbitrary, undemocratic thing. In Christ's parable of the talents, the master at random gives his three servants one, two, and five talents. The latter two servants work mightily, but limited by their "raw talent" produce four and ten talents respectively. If you start out with but two talents – of time, energy, intelligence, literary education, opportunity, flair – all your diligence will probably increase it to no more than four talents. And it may take ten talents to write a truly beautiful book. These are facts one accepts, then forgets about; they do not take away from your duty to work, nor from the joy of work. For there is no exact gauge for literary talent; you do not know how luminous a book you might write till you have written it.

You need luck, you need talent, and you need determination and perseverance which, finally, is crucial. "The writer's main task is to persist. Her most important imperative is to be at work," Solotaroff says. Through constant reading, writing, revision, a style is forged. To finish writing a difficult book, or to mature spiritually until you transcend your oldself as modern saints like Gandhi, or Mother Teresa, or Maximilian Kolbe, takes the stamina of a pilgrim walking across a continent, or a gold miner digging in the almost unendurable heat of the Kolar gold fields of India, his eyes on the prize.

Both writing and prayer require a strenuous attempt at detachment from our distracting world of dollars, demands, the telephone, mail, friends, false friends, and extended family – "the enemies of one's own household," Jesus calls them. The world that is too much with us. Entering the world of the imagination is like gazing into the enchanted universe of an intertidal pool in which purple sea urchins and emerald sea anemones glow, along with hermit crabs hiding in other creature's shells, and sea stars, black, white, and orange. I must tiptoe into this world – leaving behind the nagging Old World of people and their irritations, mess in the house, to-do lists, the jagged edges of life jabbing me – slowly, gingerly, like an immigrant unsure of the language, the customs, the geography of a country.

So spiritual directors suggest rituals to nudge the spirit into the presence of God – reading scripture, or breathing deeply to calm the body and concentrate thought before floating free. I offer myself absolution for the bumpy hours of easing into the zone, the priming rituals of reading great stylists until my pulse throbs in a complex rhythm I've unconsciously absorbed – or mechanically rereading the last few pages I've written to reenter the imaginative field of my piece. And then when ideas race from my neurons to my fingers, when my mind starts connecting all the scattered leaves of my universe, and I begin writing, almost instinctively, the language of literature: metaphor, imagery, alliteration, assonance, poetry, and my sentences sing, a car pulls into the driveway, my husband

and daughters are home, and I am back to my old life, blinking like Lazarus, summarily summoned from death's dark kingdom to the blithe goings-on of the everyday, to the crowd that gapes at him, quite unaware of the shadow world of beauty and terror (if Dante is to believed). I return shakily, a bit uncertainly, like one roused from a vivid dream, dazzled in the light.

Both writing and prayer are best done in the same place, at the same time. When I walk up to my familiar writing place – my armchair facing the woods – and see it waiting, quiet and ready, I start feeling calm. I feel like writing. An inner voice says, "Hurry up now; it's time." And contrary to romantic myth, a steady, scheduled life helps writers as much as it helps pray-ers. Flaubert: "It is good to be regular and orderly in your life, so that you may be violent and original in your work."

So too, the memories of the previous times we have met with God on our habitual holy ground usher us into an expectant quietness. Merton describes prayer in his accustomed sacred spot: *My chief joy is to escape to the attic of the garden house and the little broken window that looks out over the valley. There in the silence, I love the green grass. The tortured gestures of the apple trees have become part of my prayer.... So much do I love this solitude that when I walk out along the road to the old barns that stand alone, delight begins to overpower me from head to foot, and peace smiles even in the marrow of my bones."*

Praying is like talking a foreign language. The nouns and verbs in this holy terra incognita are in a softer, lower timbre – patience, quietness, humility, self-denial, or turning the other cheek. When I read the New Testament, I'm struck by this "upside-down kingdom," its reversal of the values of even good people. *Do not repay anyone evil for evil. Love your enemies; do good to those who hate you. Give secretly so that your right hand does not know what your left hand is doing. Invite those to your home who cannot invite you back.*

In our world, we trust in our ability to work, network, charm, maneuver. But "the wisdom of this world is foolishness in God's sight," the Apostle Paul says. In God's world, the person who trusts in God will be as blessed as "*a tree planted by the water that sends out its roots by the stream. It does not fear when heat comes; its leaves are always green. It has no worries in a year of drought, and never fails to bear fruit.*" Our world values action, quick success – grabbing our desire from the jaws of hostile fate, battering down doors with our will. In God's realm, we work quietly, knowing success will come according to his will, and in his perfect timing. In the world we know, we blow our own trumpet for fear that no one else will do it for us. If we try to walk Christ's way, we do not exalt ourselves, believing Jesus: "For everyone who exalts himself will be humbled, and he who humbles himself will be exalted." We wait, feeding off the wise, strong, sweet life of Jesus, God made flesh, metaphorically eating his flesh and drinking his blood. And when we glimpse the quietness and wisdom of God, and even momentarily take a God's eye view of our life, our internal chatter of anxiety and annoyance is silenced as our perspective shifts, and our spirit sings in worship.

Humility, an acceptance of unknowing, is a shortcut in both paths. "If the angel comes, it will be because you have wooed him by your grim resolve to be always a beginner," Rilke muses. I have grown as a writer through the humility that rejection brings. A publisher turns down my work, I do not get the fellowship I applied for, and I realize that my writing is probably not good enough – yet. In the first humbling, I feel I know nothing about literature or writing, nothing at all. Then I read with an alert hunger, studying again *Speak Memory* or *Midnight's Children*. I study the craft of writing; I let books on tape murmur to me at fallow moments in the car, on the treadmill. I revise my manuscript with renewed rigor, a rekindled passion for beauty. And through this starting again as a beginner with fresh joy, trying again to say in as few words as possible exactly what I mean; once more reading continually the books that are truly great, I learn, I grow; my writing changes, matures. Rejection is a disguised friend, freezing me in my onward motion, forcing me to rethink my essay, my vocation.

The support of a community strengthens one in both quests because they are counter-cultural; in fact, senseless judged by the efficient values of the marketplace. We invest much time in seeking God, without any scientific certainty that he exists, just the knowledge of the heart. And when with twentieth century rationality, I query: Do I really believe that God invaded human history 2000 years ago; walked our mountains and waters teaching, was crucified for uttering uncompromising truth; it helps me believe when I see Jesus' great insights proved true, not only in the wrinkles of my own life, but in the lives of other Christians. That joy comes not from gratifying every clamorous desire, but in silencing the frog chorus, *I, I, I,* and losing oneself in contemplating Christ and in loving – spouse, children, friends; in seeking righteousness rather than the gratifications of money or success. In my Christian friends too, I often observe increasing goodness and a slow deepening, as they are transformed from glory to glory, in the Apostle Paul's phrase. And though I do believe, deeply, as one does when faith is verified by experience, I am an existentialist Christian when assailed by doubt. I choose to believe like Puddleglum, the Marshwiggle in *The Chronicles of Narnia* who says: "I'm on Aslan's side, even if there isn't any Aslan to lead it. I'm going to live as like a Narnian as I can even if there isn't any Narnia." And so I go to my small church most Sundays to pray and worship with other believers, refiring my weary distracted heart with other's fervor.

Few writers evolve in solitude. At some point, even the martyrs of art – like Emily Dickinson, Keats or Thoreau – met other writers who shared the twin passions of the love of literature and their own ambition. It is reinforcing to have other writers in our lives to share the glow of that first publication in a literary journal for which we made fifteen dollars, but which meant that our craft had begun to take that miraculous leap from saggy, unpublishable writing to publishable, published writing. It strengthens our passion to have people to talk to about books and writing, and esoteric conditions like writer's block, who understand our anguish when the chapter, the book we worked on for so long miscarries. Our fellow-travelers bolster our conviction that our vocation, often dismissed as a pleasing hobby, an indulgence – *Oh how nice! You write! Have you published anything I might have seen?* – rather than the disciplined pursuit of an art is significant, worthwhile work for grown-up people.

Thomas Merton connects the two vocations in his essay, "Integrity." "Many poets are not poets for the same reason that many religious men are not saints: they never succeed in being themselves. They never get around to being the particular poet or the particular monk they are intended to be by God. They never become the man or the artist who is called for by all the circumstances of their lives.

They waste their years in vain efforts to be some other poet, some other saint. They wear out their minds and bodies in a hopeless endeavor to write somebody else's poems or possess somebody else's spirituality.

There can be an intense egoism in following everybody else. People are in a hurry to magnify themselves by imitating what is popular – and too lazy to think of anything better.

Hurry ruins saints as well as artists. They want quick success and they are in such haste to get it that they cannot take time to be true to themselves."

Writers begin as babies or mockingbirds – by imitating. Partly because of the mimicry involved in the extended process of finding their own voice and subject matter, many writers – consciously or unconsciously – sound like someone else while in their apprenticeship. The fashionable, with its lures of quick success or fame, tempts. However, once the writer grows in confidence and begin to tell the truth, she slowly discovers her own quirky, original voice. A distinctive style begins to shape itself. She begins to draw, truthfully, on her own ideas, convictions, emotions, family, and biography, unfashionable and squirmy though they may be, not on what has been published or is popular, and so finds the memoir that she alone can write, that is like no other memoir ever written, just as the inner geography of her life in its hills and valleys, heartbreak and delight, is like no other life. If she dips her pen into the sore of her own grief, her shame, her secrets, she will add electricity to her memoir, or to the more disguised forms of autobiographical writing like poems, novels, or short stories. Rushdie – "A writer's injuries are his strengths, and from his wounds will flow his sweetest, most startling dreams."

And from the molten lava of her own guilt, her hypocrisy, her pangs of despised love, and yes, stabs at virtue, self-forgetting love, longing for transcendence, the writer can mold powerful art – with this six inches of ivory, this postage stamp of earth. In *The Enigma of Arrival*, V.S. Naipaul describes how he tried to sound cosmopolitan when he first started to write, while striving to edit out his past in his Asian community in Trinidad, his naivete and clodhopperish inexperience, and the humiliations attendant on his transplantation to the West, not realizing that in his peasant background and behaviors lay his most authentic story. Later in his masterpiece, *A House for Mr. Biswas*, he lingers on the things he was most ashamed of. He writes, "Man and writer were the same person. But that is a writer's greatest discovery. It took time – and how much writing! – to arrive at that synthesis."

Both writing and prayer are disciplines of little things. I love this poem by Robert Francis:

> *Excellence is millimeters and not miles.*
> *From poor to good is great. From good to best is small.*
> *From almost best to best sometimes not measurable.*
> *The man who leaps the highest leaps perhaps an inch*
> *Above the runner-up. How glorious that inch*
> *And that split-second longer in the air before the fall.*

What are the millimeters from almost best to best? Spare writing with every unnecessary word shaken off the page. Details almost invisible to the rapid reader: the imagistic verb, the painterly image, a sentence that sings. Writing that in Conrad's phrase, "makes you hear, makes you feel – that is, before all, makes you *see*." So too, it's in the details of love that spiritual transformation occurs and exhibits itself – not so much in the showy dahlias and cannas, but in violets and bluebells. The Apostle Paul declares in, probably, the most famous passage in the New Testament: "If I speak in the tongues of men and of angels, but have not love, I am only a resounding gong or a clanging cymbal." He explicates the tiny virtues. "Love is patient, love is kind. It does not envy, it does not boast, it is not proud. It is not rude, it is not self-seeking, it is not easily angered, it keeps no record of wrongs."

A snide definition of a classic: a book which everyone wants to *have* read, but no one wants to actually read, today, tonight – the *Iliad* or *The Remembrance of Things Past*. We desire the blessings of God – life in its fullness, joy, peace, fruitfulness more than we desire God himself. We yearn for a book magical, lyrical, perfect, more than for the actual process of rewriting a chapter yet again, the long months and years before the finished book. And in both quests, the secret of joy is losing yourself in the pleasure of the present, in the play of words, in learning Christ, his quirky values, and imitating him.

How crass this sounds, but in both endeavors, quality springs from quantity! "If you want to pray better, you should pray more," Mother Teresa says. Somerset Maugham writes: "I venture the opinion that you cannot write well unless you write much." The more we write – if we do so critically, learning from good teachers, getting insightful feedback, reading, reading, practicing, practicing – the better we write. As loving-heartedness is the touchstone of the verity of our prayers, the market is the red light in writing. Rejection slips speak their own language. Of admonition. You are not there yet. Seize the day. Work as hard as you can.

Both writing and prayer usher us into the heart of mystery. From where do poems come? Or from where, indeed, does nature? Or God? The faces of the audience at the Geraldine Dodge Poetry Festival at which I sought a total immersion into poetry, were rapt as at a religious service. For literature partially and temporarily slakes the religious yearning for beauty, order, truth. Both disciplines are therapeutic in their search for the difficult truth that frees. Like prayer, the very act of writing calms and focuses us. Often, the difficulty lies in just settling down and doing it. As with sex or exercise or good conversation, it can be hard to get going, but once we have, it's as if we can keep going indefinitely. Good writing and good prayer, like good sex or good mothering, demand self-forgetfulness, losing ourselves in the other, our subject, our Lord. And the flow of creativity or prayer can be jammed and dammed by similar barricades – anxiety, hostility, anger, cherishing untruths, saying too many Noes.

We are lured into both by the dream, the promise of joy. The cost turns out to be more than we ever imagined: "not less than everything." We begin to experience the disappointment, doubt, rejection, agony – and the ultimate triumph of sacrifice – involved in becoming an artist. And we learn the rending cost of denying ourselves, taking up our cross daily, breaking out of the prison of the self and its incessant needs and demands, choosing small deaths, in a sense, so as to transcend ourselves and have a richer, more fruitful life. Jesus understood it: "Unless the grain of wheat falls into the ground and dies, it remains alone. But if it dies, it yields a mighty harvest."

When we train ourselves in the scriptural precept to pray constantly, trying to be continually aware of the quiet presence of Christ: a radiance, a luminosity, like the silent, ever-present ghost in old movies, a quietness begins to sink over our beings, the quietness in which creative thought is engendered. We must persist in both disciplines until they become instinctive, until we convert every thought, desire and frustration into a prayer, turning to God as naturally as a flower turns its face to the sun and the butterflies. Similarly, the writer must keep writing until this inward work, this daily creation, becomes as necessary as thinking; so essential that a day in which she has not written will seem a day in which she has not fully lived.

A Chinese saying: "From boredom to fascination." Though difficult at first, both quests lead to an awareness of joy, shimmering, pulsing through life. As I mature spiritually and psychologically, my values shift. Oh dear, they become more old-fashioned – the preciousness of the family I have chosen, my husband and my daughters; the balm of friendships; the durable self-forgetting pleasures in reading, art, nature, gardening. And writing? It remains my vocation, my duty and my desire, a precious strand in the tapestry of my life, a beloved pure note in its orchestra, a joyous obligation like those to my husband and children, who have no other wife, no other mother. And amid life's richness in the busy season – two daughters, four years old, and four months old; a career; a husband with a career; a house, a garden, a dog, friends, a life – can writing wait? At times, it will have to. And in the forge of dreams deferred, other jewels might be crafted:*ethos*, character, undergirding and lighting the *logos*, words, and *pathos*, emotions they evoke – the three elements of great art Aristotle outlines in his *Rhetoric*. Writing with wisdom, depth, power. And now, in the season of duties, as I choose books to read or subjects to write on more for the pleasure that dwelling on them will bring rather than for rewards of glitter or success, I am recovering some of the joy I'd lost in my anxious, striving, ambitious twenties.

Though the gloomy may say that the life of a writer is simply "the exchange of one level of rejection, uncertainty, and disappointment for another," persisting long enough to learn and master your craft gives you ever more of those moments of enchantment when your whole being is intensely alive; you are lost in the joy of work; sparks flash from your imagination and set the page on fire; and you read over a finished piece, and like God in the garden of Eden, behold what you have written, and – temporarily – decide that it is good.

About the Author

Anita Mathias' essays have been published widely--The Washington *Post, The London Magazine, The Virginia Quarterly Review, Commonweal, Notre Dame Magazine, America, The Christian Century, The Southwest Review, Contemporary Literary Criticism, New Letters, The Journal,* and two of HarperSanFrancisco's annual *The Best Spiritual Writing* anthologies. She has won several awards for her non-fiction including fellowships from The National Endowment for the Arts; The Minnesota State Arts Board; The Jerome Foundation, The Vermont Studio Center; The Virginia Center for the Creative Arts, and the First Prize for the Best General Interest Article from the Catholic Press Association of the United States and Canada.

Anita has a B.A. and M.A. in English from Somerville College, Oxford University and an M.A. in Creative Writing (with a creative thesis in Poetry) from the Ohio State University. She has taught Creative Writing at the College of William and Mary and at regional writers' conferences in the United States, but now lives in Oxford, England, with her husband Roy and her young daughters, Zoe and Irene.

You may order further copies of *Wandering Between Two Worlds* from the author's website **www.anitamathias.com**

or from the Publisher

Benediction Books
The White Cottage,
11 Kiln Lane,
Garsington,
Oxford
OX44 9AR
United Kingdom
benedictionbooks@btinternet.com

via this order form:

Please send me .... copies of *Wandering Between Two Worlds: Essays on Art and Faith by Anita Mathias.*

I enclose a UK bank cheque for .... payable to Anita Mathias for .... copies at £7.99 each.

Name	....
Address	....
	....
City	....
Country	....
Postcode/ZIP	....
E-mail	....

Please allow a week for delivery. Do not send cash. We do not share or sell our customer's details.

☐ Please tick here if you DO NOT want to receive further information from Benediction Books.

Made in United States
Orlando, FL
05 July 2022

19444959R00085